NOW AND THEN

Reading and Writing
about the
American Immigrant Experience

....

Neil Reich

Queensborough Community College,
City University of New York
and
Eastern District High School,
New York City Board of Education

St. Martin's Press
New York

....

. . . .

MANAGER, PUBLISHING SERVICES: Emily Berleth
PROJECT EDITOR, PUBLISHING SERVICES: Kalea Chapman
PROJECT MANAGEMENT: Books By Design, Inc.
PRODUCTION SUPERVISOR: Dennis Para
TEXT DESIGN: Books By Design, Inc.
COVER DESIGN: Rod Hernandez
COVER PHOTO: *Right:* Woodfin Camp & Associates, Inc. *Left:* UPI/Bettmann

Library of Congress Catalog Card Number: 94-80108

0 9 8 7 6
f e d c b a

For information, write:

St. Martin's Press, Inc.
175 Fifth Avenue
New York, NY 10010

ISBN: 0-312-11982-8

Photo credits

Page 5: Hector Acebes/Photo Researchers, Inc.; Page 21: Magnus Bartlett/Woodfin Camp & Associates; Page 35: Wide World Photos, Inc.; Page 47: Spencer Grant/Stock Boston; Page 61: Tom McCarthy/The Picture Cube; Page 79: HMS Images, © 1994/The Image Bank; Page 93: Wide World Photos, Inc.; Page 111: Bob Daemmrich/Stock Boston; Page 135: Richard Hutchings/Photo Researchers, Inc.; Page 149: Fredrik D. Bodin/Stock Boston; Page 163: W.W. Thompson III/The Image Bank; Page 185: Paul S. Conklin/PhotoEdit.

Acknowledgments

Acknowledgments and copyrights are continued at the back of the book on page 216, which constitutes an extension of the copyright page.

It is a violation of the law to reproduce these selections by any means whatsoever without the written permission of the copyright holder.

Selected excerpts from *The Boat of Longing* by O. E. Rölvaag. Copyright 1933 by Harper & Brothers. Copyright renewed 1960 by Harper & Brothers. Reprinted by permission of HarperCollins Publishers, Inc.

Excerpt from *The Emigrants* by Vilhelm Moberg. Copyright © 1951 by Vilhelm Moberg. Reprinted by permission of The Estate of Vilhelm Moberg.

. . . .

Dedicated
to the
loving memory
of my
father,

HY REICH,

1928–1976

CONTENTS

. . . .

. . . .

CHAPTER 7   PHOTOGRAPHS *93*

. . . .

. . . .

. . . .

. . . .

PREFACE

Now and Then brings together published literature and authentic student essays related to the American immigrant experience. Students read, respond to, and analyze the work of professional and student writers and produce their own full-length essays. The book is intended for high-intermediate and advanced students of English as a second language in college and high school.

The readings—from a wide range of American literature written by and about immigrants to the United States—chronicle more than a century and a half of migration to the United States from Europe, Asia, and the Americas.*

The student essays—motivated by the readings—were written by high school seniors and college freshmen and are the final products of the process approach to writing emphasized throughout the book. The essays have been revised, often several times, by the student writers. As with all published material, any remaining errors in grammar, spelling, and punctuation have been edited and corrected.

The key features of *Now and Then* include:

High-Interest Material. The theme of immigration as a basis of ESL instruction is a logical choice, both for the immigrant who has come to settle in the United States and for the foreign student who will return home after a period of study: it is the experience that almost all ESL students have in common. Students are motivated by and respond to the narratives and themes, which reflect their own experiences.

Thematic Organization. In keeping with current whole language pedagogy, the instructional material is organized into chapters built around a unifying theme related to the immigrant experience. Thus, instructors may choose to work through the book from beginning to end or cover selected chapters, as determined by time constraints and the needs and interests of the students.

---

*The background information about the immigrant groups mentioned in this book comes from *The Harvard Encyclopedia of American Ethnic Groups,* ed. Stephen Thernstrom et al. (Cambridge: Harvard University Press, 1980).

The Use of Authentic Student Essays. Student writing is recognized not only for its quality but for its instructional value as well. Because student writing is so accessible in its content, organization, and technique, successful essays serve as effective models to motivate and instruct other student writers.

The Process Approach to Writing. Writing instruction is based on a process approach that helps students generate ideas, write, and revise to produce full-length essays.

The Transition from Personal Writing to Academic Writing. Initially, students write about familiar experiences. As academic writing is introduced, the skills developed through personal writing are transferred to the more formal types of academic writing required in content area courses.

Reading-Writing Connection. The connection between the development of reading and writing proficiency is recognized as equal attention is given to both skills in an integrated fashion through many interrelated activities.

The Exploration of Literature. To promote an appreciation of literature, students are encouraged to explore personal responses and to analyze content, organization, and technique.

User-Friendly Format. The uniform format of each chapter provides the basis of a consistent routine of study. The material may be easily broken down into segments appropriate for the allotted daily or weekly class time.

Reinforcement of Material. As students gain greater facility with writing, they are encouraged to revise their essays. Similarly, numerous activities suggest that students return to readings in earlier chapters and re-examine texts to discover aspects that may previously have gone unnoticed.

Organization

Now and Then is organized into twelve chapters, each with a unifying theme:

Leaving Home

The Journey

First Days

Learning English

Culture

Changes

Photographs

Friends and Family

At School

Places

At Work

Issues in the News

After the Introduction, the chapters of *Now and Then* follow a similar format: Each chapter begins with an introductory note. A key question about the students' own experiences encourages immediate personal involvement with the theme explored in the chapter. Following the introductory note, each chapter is organized in four main sections, with subsections within, as follows: Reading, Student Essay, Focus on Writing, and Essay Writing.

. . . .

READING

Students begin to examine the theme of the chapter by reading and analyzing a piece of professional writing. The reading selection is explored through several different activities:

Establishing the Context. This section provides a brief historical sketch and background information on the immigrant group featured in the reading selection.

To Begin. This section is designed to promote active reading of the literature and serves as a foundation for discussion and/or written response.

Reading Selections. The multicultural readings explore the themes highlighted in the chapters.

Response and Analysis. These activities encourage personal response to and analysis of the reading selection.

Further Exploration of Language and Literature. This section covers topics such as symbolism; historical and literary references; figurative and literal language; simile and metaphor; alliteration; standard and nonstandard language; fact vs. opinion; and other techniques.

Vocabulary. A vocabulary activity focuses on determining meaning from context.

. . . .

STUDENT ESSAY

This section presents an authentic student essay related to the theme of the chapter. Each student essay is accompanied by a response and analysis section, which encourages personal response to and analysis of the student essay and develops strategies for peer revision.

. . . .

FOCUS ON WRITING

This section focuses on ways in which other student writers have produced successful essays. Topics include journal writing; an introduction to the writing process; developing vs. omitting material; direct quotation vs. reported speech; choosing the title; the introduction; organizing ideas; explaining references; the conclusion; peer revision; interviewing; and library research. This material is reviewed and reinforced throughout the text. After exploration of writing on personal themes, the text addresses formal academic writing.

. . . .

ESSAY WRITING

Here students have the opportunity to employ the elements of successful writing presented in the book.

Generating Ideas. This presents a number of strategies designed to help students generate ideas for their own essays.

Assignment. The culmination comes with the assignment of an essay topic related to the chapter theme.

Acknowledgments

Although I am not able to thank all the people who have helped make this book a reality, I would like to acknowledge a few.

I begin by expressing deep appreciation to my wonderful students. They continue to enrich my life and make my job so enjoyable.

Special thanks go to two friends and colleagues: Marion Halberg of the New York City Board of Education and the New York City Writing Project at Lehman College for her continuous input from the start of this project to its completion and Steven Haber of Jersey City State College for sharing his expertise on student writing.

At St. Martin's Press, I am indebted to my acquiring editor Naomi Silverman for her belief in the book and to Carl Whithaus, my editor, for his easy availability and his expert guidance.

I thank my many colleagues at Eastern District High School. Special thanks go to our principal, Louis LaBosco, and to Robert LiPetri, Chairman of the Foreign Language/ESL Department for their tireless support, to Educational Assistants Patricia Gavilánez, Eunice Vásquez, and Veronica Alvarado for their work with student writers, and to school librarians Shirley Blank, Nelly Rodríguez, and Mitchell Bobrick, presently of the Palm Beach County, Florida, School System.

In the Basic Skills Department at Queensborough Community College, I thank Paul Panes, Jerrold Nudelman, and Elaine Morton for the help they gave to a new colleague and Francine Stavis for her many acts of kindness.

I thank the many good people at Books By Design for their help with the production of the book: Nancy Benjamin, project editor; Sally Bindari, designer; and Gabriel Weiss, copyeditor.

I thank my mother Mickey and her husband Sandy for keeping an eye on the kids and my brother Ken for his guidance on computer matters.

I would like to thank the following reviewers for their insights and suggestions: Karen Einstein, Santa Rosa Junior College; Steven Haber, Jersey City State College; Marion Halberg, New York City Board of Education and NYC Writing Project at Lehman College, CUNY; David MacWilliams, Vanderbilt University; Gay Washburn, University of Pennsylvania; and P. Fawn Whittaker, Brigham Young University–Hawaii.

Most of all, however, I am grateful to my wife Yael, my daughter Hadas, and my son Ben. Thanks for everything.

Neil Reich

INTRODUCTION

The United States is a country of immigrants. With the exception of the native American and the descendant of the African slave, every American has either immigrated to the United States or is descended from someone who has. Since the first records were compiled in 1820, more than 60 million men, women, and children from almost every place on earth have left their homelands to come to live in the United States. And every year hundreds of thousands of others continue the tradition. Although about 700,000 visas are set aside annually for the purpose of legal immigration, many persons enter without the required documentation. Some are granted legal status as refugees who have a well-founded fear of persecution back home. While most will remain, others will work or study for a time and return to the lands of their birth.

The purpose of this book is to help you improve your English—particularly your ability to read and write, skills necessary for leading a fuller life in school, in the workplace, even at home. To help you improve your English, you will read, respond to, and analyze stories by and about others who have lived the immigrant experience, and you will also write your own.

. . . .

KEEPING A JOURNAL

Let's begin with an activity that may already be familiar to you: keeping a journal. When you make entries in a journal, you are free to write about anything. You might write about matters related to your personal life, observations about the world around you, topics in the news, or anything that happens to be on your mind. Throughout this book, you will be asked to respond to the issues raised in the readings. While you might want to discuss these with your classmates, you might also consider using them as topics for your journal.

At this point, don't be overly concerned with spelling, grammar, punctuation, or organization. With journal writing the emphasis is not on how or what you write but rather that you write for some time every day. If you are unclear as to what you might like to write in your journal, the following journal entries—written by other ESL students—might be helpful.

. . . .

SAMPLE JOURNAL ENTRIES

9/15

Bob took me to his house on Long Island today. We brought some food and went to the beach. I was surprised that so many people were walking near the ocean. I didn't realize that the beach could be so beautiful in the fall. Before I had gone to the beach only in the summer. We looked at the huge sun which had many colors: orange, yellow, red. It looked like a beautiful picture. . . .

1/9

The other day in my English class we were discussing the conflicts which immigrants and their children feel, the conflict between becoming American and maintaining the native language and culture. I thought of my friend Maggie. When I look at her, I begin to think how fast the Chinese culture can disappear. Her parents are Chinese who came to the United States twenty years ago. Maggie was born here, but her parents speak Chinese at home. It doesn't matter. She spends most of her time at school with her American friends, watching American television, going to American movies, listening to American music, reading American magazines. Her English is far better than her Chinese. She never went to Chinese school and is not able to write and read our language. I know if she marries an American guy the Chinese culture will not be given to the children, and they will know nothing of our traditions.

5/7

Yesterday my friend and I went to see a movie, *My Family/Mi Familia,* about a Mexican American family in California. In the 1920s, the father, José Sanchez, walks all the way from his village in central Mexico to stay with a relative in Los Angeles. He marries and raises six children. The film tells many different stories from the lives of the parents and their children over the next 50 years. One son becomes a successful lawyer; another gets involved with a gang and is killed. One daughter becomes a nun; another opens a fancy restaurant. All the while, the father works as a gardener in the homes of the rich people on the other side of town. For me the saddest part of the movie was when the wife of one of the sons, an immigrant from El Salvador, dies while giving birth to a baby boy. The boy's father ends up in jail and doesn't see his son for several years. I was happy when the boy and his father are reunited at the end. It was a really good movie, like life, both happy and sad.

....

ANALYSIS

What sorts of topics have these students chosen to write about in their journals?

....

JOURNAL ASSIGNMENT

For your first journal entry, you might describe your feelings and thoughts as you begin this course. It may be helpful to consider these questions:

How are you feeling as you begin this ESL course?

Describe some of the things you especially liked or disliked about your other ESL courses.

Are you satisfied with your progress in learning English?

What do you hope to accomplish in this course?

Try writing for several minutes. Remember, at this point, don't be overly concerned with spelling, grammar, punctuation, or organization. Just try to explore your feelings and thoughts. After you have completed your entry, look over what you have written. You might find that you would like to add more to your entry.

Try writing in your journal every day for ten or fifteen minutes. Although your journal is for your personal use, at times you might want to share what you have written with your teacher or a friend. Like other students, with time you will probably look forward to those quiet moments when you reflect and write in your journal.

Throughout this course and beyond, you might use your journals to note your feelings and thoughts about coming from another country to live in the United States. As you work through this book, compare your own experiences with those of the immigrants of today and yesterday.

LEAVING
HOME

. . . .

As you read this, throughout the world men, women, and children are making the final preparations for their trip to the United States. What do you recall of the day you left home?

READING FROM

The Boat of Longing

O. E. RÖLVAAG

. . . .

ESTABLISHING THE CONTEXT

In recent decades immigration from Norway to the United States has not been substantial; no more than a few hundred Norwegians come here each year. As with many of the other nations of Europe, Norwegian immigration reached its high point generations ago. Between 1860 and 1930, more than three quarters of a million Norwegians—an extremely large number for a country with a relatively small population—settled in the United States. In fact, during those years, Norway contributed a higher proportion of its population to settlement in the United States than any country other than Ireland.

In 1896, at age twenty, Ole Edvart Rölvaag left his small village in northern Norway to come to the United States, joining thousands of his compatriots. Eventually settling in Minnesota, Rölvaag dedicated his life to telling the story of the Norwegian Americans and to the preservation of their language and culture. In the excerpt from Rölvaag's novel *The Boat of Longing,* Nils Vaag, a young Norwegian fisherman, is leaving his elderly mother and father to seek his fortune in America. The three are walking to the general store of their small village. There the young man will catch a ferry that will take him to a steamship on the first part of his trip across the Atlantic.

. . . .

TO BEGIN

Read only the first and last paragraphs of the selection, skipping the middle. Both these paragraphs are *narrative;* that is, they tell a story. The middle section contains *dialogue,* the words that the *characters* or people in the story say. Without reading the middle section, try to anticipate the dialogue that takes place among the father, mother, and son. After you have completed the reading, you will be able to compare the dialogue you anticipated with the dialogue in the text.

You will probably come across some unfamiliar words in this excerpt from *The Boat of Longing.* However, you can still enjoy and understand what you read without knowing the definition of every word. It is often possible to guess at the definition of an unfamiliar word or phrase by its *context,* the surrounding words and sentences. Read for your interest and pleasure about the moment Nils leaves home. Don't be overly concerned with words and phrases you don't understand; there will be a vocabulary activity after you read, respond to, and analyze the selection.

FROM

THE BOAT OF LONGING

O. E. RÖLVAAG

Presently all three were outside in the rain. A little way up the path Nils had to turn around for a last look at the place and the sea. He stopped. 1

"Better tie the boat more securely, Father; she'll be bad tonight. Or would you like me to do it? We've plenty of time." 2

But the father didn't stop, and so they walked on. 3

From the three trudging figures there came no sound save the steady beat of their footfalls. The west storm screamed about their ears. The wet heather pasted itself stickily to their legs. 4

Within sight of Jörgensen's store Nils drew to a halt. 5

"You mustn't come any farther," he said. 6

"No," replied Jo. 7

"No," echoed Mother Anna, hollowly, "we'll not go any farther now." 8

Nils stretched forth his hand—to the father first. 9

"Thanks for—!" But that was all he could muster. From the strong face before him two gleaming eyes peered at him through the rain. So stolid and shut was the look of the face in that instant that to say what thoughts worked behind it would have baffled the most expert reader of minds. 10

The father took the hand, locked it hard for a moment, then dropped it; but not a sound escaped his lips. 11

Nils offered his hand to his mother. She grasped it, clung desperately to it, could not let it go. The hand not being enough, she seized his arm, caught him close, and began to cry so convulsively that she sank upon his shoulder. 12

"Oh—my boy, my boy! . . . My blessed boy! . . . God reward you for the comfort you've been! . . . And God be—!" 13

Nils held her until her crying, having stilled itself, came more easily,   14
like a child's.

Then with a wrench he tore himself loose and went.   15

Have got a little way off, he had to look back. This he had not   16
wanted to do, but he couldn't help it.

And there through the shrieking storm and driving rain he saw the   17
figure of his mother, plain as could be against the murky sky; but not his
father's. The mother was holding her right hand high. . . . He walked
on, only to turn again. The figure had not moved . . . stood there as before, pointing skyward. The gloom and the rain were now so thick that
the hand could no longer be distinguished . . . only the arm reaching up
into darkness.

. . . .

RESPONSE AND ANALYSIS

1. Write for a few minutes in response to what you have read. Besides summarizing,
   you may want to explore your feelings and thoughts about the reading. (Two
   responses written by other students appear in the "Sample Responses" section
   below.) It may be helpful to consider these categories:
   a. what you understood about the reading
   b. something that puzzled you in the reading
   c. something you would like to discuss with the writer or one of the characters
   d. a memory the reading evoked
   e. how you felt about the reading

2. Compare the dialogue in the text with the dialogue you anticipated. How were
   they similar? How were they different?

3. Working with your classmates in small groups, read the story aloud. Have different group members take the parts of the father, mother, son, and *narrator*, or
   storyteller.

4. As the father and son part, the older man's look is described as "so stolid and shut
   . . . that to say what thoughts worked behind it would have baffled the most expert
   reader of minds." Using your own experiences as well as what you have learned in
   school and from other sources, discuss what the two men might have been thinking at that moment.

5. Contrast the behavior of the father and the mother at the departure of their son.

···············

SAMPLE RESPONSES

When I read the story I felt like it was happening to me. I thought about the day I left my country, my friends, and my family. It's hard for us to leave everything we love. But we have the dream that one day we will go back and see our family and friends again. Americans don't realize all we have lost in order to come here. They don't think about how sad we are to leave our loved ones. Sometimes we suffer so not knowing if we will ever be able to go back. In my own experiences, I've seen that our parents have tried to give us a better life, but it's difficult for them. They are not prepared to get a good job. They send us to school to study to have a profession because they don't want us to suffer like them. At least I came here with my family and we are together. I can't imagine going through what Nils went through . . . or his parents. I felt sad when I read the story, but I have to say that this is real life.

I can't understand why the father didn't say anything to his son. I would like to ask that man why he showed no emotion. If he was my son I would tell him how much I was going to miss him. I would tell him how much I love him, and to write me if he needs anything. The father didn't say anything. Unbelievable! If it was my father who acted that way, I would have felt bad. The father acts as if Nils is going away on a short trip for a couple of days.

···············

FURTHER EXPLORATION OF LANGUAGE AND LITERATURE: SYMBOLISM

The first sentence of the reading immediately notes that "all three were outside in the rain." Throughout the story, there are many other references to the rain. List as many as you can find. What do they add to the story?

One answer might be found in the concept of *symbolism*. A *symbol* is commonly defined as "an object in the physical world which represents an idea, feeling, or other abstract quality." Some students have commented that the reason Rölvaag has included so much description of the rain and storm is to reflect the sadness and confusion involved in the separation of the family. In other words, the rain and the storm—which exist in the physical world—are symbols of sadness and confusion, which are abstract ideas.

Another symbol might be found in the last sentence of the reading: "The gloom and the rain were now so thick that the hand could no longer be distinguished . . . only the arm reaching up into darkness." We know that the day is dark because of the storm. What might the description of the mother's arm "reaching up into darkness" symbolize?

. . . .

VOCABULARY

In the following passages, try to determine the meaning of each underlined word by its context. (You may want to choose additional words from the reading if you found the vocabulary very challenging.) Then provide a dictionary definition either in English or in your native language. Finally, read the excerpt from *The Boat of Longing* a second time, paying close attention to the words you have learned as well as the other points discussed in the previous activities.

1. From the three <u>trudging</u> figures there came no sound save the steady beat of their footfalls.

2. Within sight of Jörgensen's store Nils drew to a <u>halt.</u>

3. From the strong face before him two gleaming eyes <u>peered</u> at him through the rain.

4. So <u>stolid</u> and shut was the look of the face in that instant that to say what thoughts worked behind it would have <u>baffled</u> the most expert reader of minds.

5. She grasped it, <u>clung</u> desperately to it, could not let it go.

6. And there through the <u>shrieking</u> storm and driving rain he saw the figure of his mother, plain as could be against the <u>murky</u> sky . . .

7. The <u>gloom</u> and the rain were now so thick that the hand could no longer be distinguished . . .

Student Essay

Taking the subway to school one day, Eric Guzmán from Honduras recalled the day he left home to come to the United States.

RIDING ON A LONELY TRAIN

ERIC GUZMÁN

The other day I was riding on the "L" train on my way to school. It   1
was about 7:00 in the morning. I was standing by the door because
there were three homeless men sprawled out on the seats. When the

train stopped at the Sutter Avenue station, an old man with a trumpet got on. He started to play. It was a sad tune; I think it was what Americans call "the blues." It was only me, the three homeless men, and the old man blowing the blues on his horn there on the train. For some reason, I was reminded of a sad day in my life years ago.

It was March 29, 1988. It was 8:00 in the morning when my mother   2
woke me up. I had to finish packing my bags because I had to leave Honduras. My father and I were moving to the United States. I was coming here in order to get a better education than I could in my country. By 10:00, I was at the kitchen table drinking a strong cup of sweet black coffee. My mother and I sat in silence.

The car that would take me to the airport had arrived. A thousand   3
sad thoughts accompanied me in the car on that short ride to the airport. There I met my father, who had come earlier. The flight would leave shortly. I said goodbye to my mother. The tears that rolled down her cheeks mixed with my own. "Take care of yourself, my son," she said. "Study hard and make your mother proud."

I boarded the plane, sat down, and looked through the window, tears   4
blurring my vision. I couldn't believe that I was leaving my beautiful country. I wished that I could run off the plane but I knew that I couldn't. Soon the plane was up in the air, on its way to New York City. . . .

The train stopped and the conductor opened the doors. The trumpet   5
player got off. Speaking only to myself, I said, "It was wise to come to the United States. Here I have more opportunities. Someday I will bring my mother to live here with me."

. . . .

RESPONSE AND ANALYSIS

1. Think of the day you left your homeland. How does it compare with this account?

2. Look at the first line of paragraph 2: "It was March 29, 1988." Eric understands that he must anticipate questions a reader might have and provide the *background information* in order to make his narrative clear. In this case, the reader might wonder, "When did this take place?" Later in the paragraph Eric mentions that he was leaving Honduras. Again, without this information, the reader might ask, "What country was he leaving?" What other background information has Eric provided?

3. *Setting* refers to where and when the action of a story takes place. How does the setting change throughout this essay?

4. When Eric wrote the first version or *draft* of his essay, he included only paragraphs 2, 3, and 4. Later, he decided to add paragraphs 1 and 5. What does the addition of these paragraphs contribute to the essay?

5. In paragraph 3, Eric writes, "A thousand sad thoughts accompanied me. . . . " List some of the thoughts he might have had at the time. Would you have preferred if Eric had mentioned some of them? Explain.

6. *Direct quotation* refers to the use of the exact words a person says. List the direct quotations Eric uses in the essay. Of all the words that were exchanged on the day he left home, Eric chose to include only a brief sentence or two. Why do you think these were particularly memorable? What specific words do you recall from the day you left home?

7. Eric ends his essay by expressing a sense of optimism about living in the United States: "Here I have more opportunities." What feelings might the three homeless men have toward their homeland? Toward immigrants like Eric?

Focus on Writing: The Writing Process

When you read a well-written piece such as Eric's, it is easy to forget that the essay is the final product of a process that involves a number of steps. Eric first generated ideas about the topic. Then he wrote his first draft. Having written his first draft, Eric carefully reread his essay. In addition to checking for errors in grammar, sentence structure, and spelling—a process called *proofreading*—Eric decided that he was not completely satisfied with his essay and so began the *revision*. When you revise your writing you consider ways to change its content and organization. In Eric's case, he decided to add the first and last paragraphs.

. . . .

FROM FIRST DRAFT TO REVISED ESSAY

Later in this chapter, you will have the opportunity to generate ideas for your own essay. For now, let's examine some elements that are found in effective writing as well as some issues involved in revising a first draft to make it even more successful. Here are two versions of an essay written by Pedro Batista about the day he left the Dominican Republic.

LEAVING HOME
(Early Draft)
PEDRO BATISTA

I can still remember the last day I was in Santo Domingo. It was a 1
very sad day. All my relatives and friends had come by to wish us a successful trip. At that moment I was supposed to be happy, but instead of
being happy, I was awfully sad. In fact, I can now say that it was the
saddest day in my life. Although I was going to the United States with
my immediate family, I was leaving my grandmother, aunts, cousins,
and friends.

While I was packing my bags, I was thinking about how wonderful it 2
would be to stay home and not go to the United States. As I went to put
the bags in the car that would take us to the airport, I stopped in the
middle of the street and observed the neighborhood which had been
my home for almost my whole life. I started remembering all the good
things that I had gone through.

The final moment had arrived. I felt like crying to see all the people 3
saying goodbye. We got in the car and I took a final look at the neighborhood and the people I will never forget, people who were kind to
me throughout the years.

On the way to the airport, my mother told me how hard Father had 4
fought to make this happen and that we couldn't disappoint him. My
mother meant that I should think about the life my father was trying to
give me in the United States, where I could have a chance to study. We
arrived at the airport and got on the plane. On the way to the United
States, I was thinking that maybe there would be better opportunities for
me there. I promised myself that one day I would return to Santo
Domingo as a successful person.

As you read the revised essay, note the differences between the two versions. Afterward you will be able to analyze why Pedro decided to make these changes.

LEAVING HOME
(Revised Essay)
PEDRO BATISTA

I can still remember the last day that I was in Santo Domingo. It was 1
a sad day. All my relatives and friends had come by to wish us a suc-

cessful trip. At that moment I was supposed to be happy, but instead of being happy I was awfully sad. In fact, I can now say that it was the saddest day in my life. Although I was going to the United States with my immediate family, I was leaving my grandmother, aunts, cousins, and friends.

While I was packing my bags, I was thinking about how wonderful it 2
would be to stay home and not go to the United States. As I went to put the bags in the car that would take us to the airport, I stopped in the middle of the street and observed the whole neighborhood which had been my home for almost my whole life. I started remembering all the good things that I had gone through. The first thing that came to my mind was all the games that I played with my friends, especially the one that we call *el tapao.* We would run all around the neighborhood. I suppose that's why I remembered it as I looked around. Later I learned that kids in the United States play a similar game called "tag."

The final moment had arrived. We got in the car and I took a last 3
look at the neighborhood and the people I will never forget, people who were nice to me throughout the years. I recalled the time I was four or five years old and had gotten lost. A kind stranger brought me back to my worried parents. I thought about our neighbor Lucinda, a heavy woman with three children and no husband. How many times had she sent over one of her kids to borrow some cooking oil or rice!

On the way to the airport, my mother said, "Your father has fought a 4
lot to make this happen, and we are not going to disappoint him." My mother wanted me to think about the life my father was trying to give me where I could have a chance to study.

We arrived at the airport and got on the plane. On the way to the 5
United States, I was thinking that maybe there would be better opportunities there. One day I would return to Santo Domingo as a successful person.

. . . .

ANALYSIS

1. In paragraph 2 of the early draft, Pedro writes, "I started remembering all the good things that I had gone through." As he reread his first draft, Pedro decided that he could better convey his sense of loss about leaving his friends by giving an example of the kinds of activities they used to engage in. What example did he add in the revised essay?

2. In paragraph 3 of the early draft, Pedro writes, " . . . I took a final look at the neighborhood and the people I will never forget." Again he decided to be more specific. He added two brief *anecdotes* or short personal stories. List these.

3. In the last paragraph of the early draft, Pedro relates a part of the conversation he and his mother had in the car ride to the airport. He does this through *reported speech*—that is, he summarizes the conversation without using the exact words that were spoken. How does he relate the conversation in the revised essay?

As noted, when you revise your writing, you are concerned with its content and organization. Revision may involve a number of changes: you may decide to add details, examples, or anecdotes. Or you may decide to eliminate unimportant or irrelevant material. Sometimes as you reread your essay, you may realize that you have not provided sufficient background material to make your intended meaning clear. Or you may decide to change the organization and move material from one part of the essay to another.

. . . .

USING A WORD PROCESSOR

Try to do your writing on a word processor. These are often available at school or in the library. A word processor allows you to save your writing on the computer's hard drive or on a floppy disk so that you can work on it later. As you go back and revise your writing and decide to add text, eliminate passages, or change the organization of the material, you won't have to spend time and energy copying large parts that will remain unchanged. You can concentrate on only those parts you would like to revise. Without the tedious task of copying, you will probably look forward to revising your writing as you take pride in the final product.

In addition, most word processing programs have spelling and grammar checks. These point out words you may have misspelled or errors in grammar you may have made, even suggesting possible correct alternatives. Such features can help you with your proofreading while you gain greater technical mastery of English.

Like most things in life, the more satisfaction you derive from your writing, the more you enjoy doing it. And the more you enjoy writing, the more you will want to do it, thus becoming an even better writer. If you haven't used a word processor before, the going might be a little slow in the beginning. You'll soon get accustomed to it, and when you do, you'll wonder how you were ever able to do without one.

Now read two versions of an essay written by Agnes Kossut, a young woman who left her parents and younger brother in Poland to further her education in the United States. Like Eric and Pedro, Agnes was not entirely satisfied with the early draft and so made a number of changes.

LEAVING HOME
(Early Draft)

AGNES KOSSUT

I didn't know much about life in the United States. I was just so   1
happy about the possibility of coming to live in New York. I had always
liked to learn languages. Therefore I thought that being in school with
American people would give me the opportunity to learn English very
fast. This consideration made me strong and gave me the courage to
make this difficult decision.

I remember that all my friends were envious of me that I had the op-   2
portunity to come to the United States, the country which for Poles was
connected with things wonderful and amazing. After some time my
friends noticed that I was upset and asked me about it. Yes, it was true;
when I had gotten my visa and when I had the plane ticket in my hand,
all my enthusiasm began to disappear. Some people may not understand why, but the answer is really simple. I began to be afraid, really
afraid. My feelings had begun to change. I began to regret my decision.

August 18. I didn't want my parents to recognize that I wasn't happy.   3
I knew that the situation was painful for them, too, especially since I am
their only daughter. They wanted the best for me. My father knew that
in the United States I could get a better education and I could learn English well. They were thinking about my future and my career.

It was time for me to go. It was the most unhappy and terrible day in   4
my life. I said goodbye to my friends, who were still envious of me. I
looked at my house for the last time and I went into the car. During the
trip to Warsaw, my parents and I tried to talk but to no avail. My mother
just said, "Why have we done this? Is education worth all this pain?"

I recall those last five minutes at the airport. I didn't want to prolong   5
this painful situation. I forced a smile on my face. My parents knew that
it was time to say goodbye. They hugged me and kissed me with a parent's love. My mother didn't want me to suffer. They told me that they
would phone me every week and write me often. I turned and began to
go to my gate fast. Suddenly I stopped. I wanted to tell my parents how
much I loved them. People stared at me but I didn't know if my parents
saw me or not. I disappeared into the crowd.

Again as you read the revised essay, note the differences between the two versions. Afterward you will be able to analyze why Agnes decided to make these revisions.

LEAVING HOME
(Revised Essay)

AGNES KOSSUT

I didn't know much about life in the United States. I was just so happy about the possibility of coming to live in New York. I had always liked to learn languages. Therefore I thought that being in school with American people would give me the opportunity to learn English very fast. This consideration made me strong and gave me the courage to make this difficult decision.

I remember that all my friends were envious of me that I had the opportunity to come to the United States, the country which for Poles was connected with things wonderful and amazing. After some time my friends asked me, "Why are you so upset? How can a person be unhappy in this situation?" Yes, it was true; when I had gotten my visa and when I had the plane ticket in my hand, all my enthusiasm began to disappear. Some people may not understand why, but the answer is really simple. I began to be afraid, really afraid. My feelings had begun to change. I asked myself, "What have I done? How will life be without my loving parents?" But I couldn't find answers to these questions.

I didn't want my parents to recognize that I wasn't happy. I knew that the situation was painful for them, too, especially since I am their only daughter. They wanted the best for me. My father knew that in the United States I could get a better education and I could learn English well. They were thinking about my future and my career.

August 18. It was the most unhappy and terrible day in my life. I said goodbye to my friends, who were still envious of me. I looked at my house for the last time and I went into the car. During the trip to Warsaw, where there is an international airport, my parents and I tried to talk but to no avail. Nobody could directly face the fact that I was truly leaving. Then my six-year-old brother hugged me and asked, "Who will play with me? Who will watch cartoons on TV with me when my sister leaves us?" I tried to explain that I was going to be back home after one year, but at this moment I couldn't bear the situation any longer. Big tears appeared on my cheeks and my little brother began to cry louder and louder. Nobody could stop him. Suddenly my mother turned and said, "Why have we done this? Is education worth all this pain?"

I recall those last five minutes at the airport. I didn't want to prolong this painful situation. I forced a smile on my face. I took my brother in my hands and I said that when I come back I would bring him an expensive "Police Lego," something he was dreaming about, along with a big bag of American candy. I was happy when his sad face quickly brightened.

My parents knew that it was time to say goodbye. They hugged me and kissed me with a parent's love. My mother didn't want me to suffer. She whispered, "Don't worry, my little daughter. Try to be happy and believe that you will find wonderful friends." They told me that they would phone me every weekend and write me often.   6

I turned and began to go to the gate fast. Suddenly I stopped. I wanted to tell my parents how much I loved them. People stared at me but I didn't know if my parents saw me or not. I disappeared into the crowd.   7

. . . .

ANALYSIS

Make a list of the changes Agnes has made in the revised essay and explain why you think she made them. Use these terms to help your analysis: *anecdote, example, quotation,* and *background information.*

Essay Writing

. . . .

GENERATING IDEAS

Like most writers, you will probably want to generate ideas for your essay before you write the first draft. One way to do this is to think about your topic and make notes as you come up with ideas. Use the questions below as a guide, but feel free to consider anything related to the topic.

a. Where do you come from?

b. When did you leave?

c. How old were you?

d. How did you feel at the time?

e. Who accompanied you on the trip?

f. What kind of transportation did you take?

g. Did anyone come to see you off?

h. How did you say goodbye?

i. Does something you did or saw or thought about on that day stand out in your mind? Describe it.

j. What was the most memorable thing someone said to you that day?

k. Looking back, how do you feel about that day now?

. . . .

ASSIGNMENT

Use the ideas you generated in the previous activity as the basis of an essay about the day you left your homeland to come to the United States. Keep in mind the elements that Eric, Pedro, and Agnes used in their successful essays: specific anecdotes, sufficient background information, and direct quotation. After you have written an early draft of your essay, share it with a teacher or a friend and explore possible revisions that would make it even more successful.

2

THE
JOURNEY

· · · · · · · · · · · · · · · ·

Hundreds of thousands of men, women, and children continue to make their way to the United States each year, following in the footsteps of those who have come before. What do you recall of your own journey?

READING FROM

The Emigrants

VILHELM MOBERG

· · · · · · · · · · · · · · · ·

ESTABLISHING THE CONTEXT

Like their neighbors from Norway, immigrants from Sweden made their way to the United States in substantial numbers generations ago. As early as the 1840s, the promise of free farmland had already lured thousands of Swedes to the New World. During the nineteenth century and the first decades of the twentieth, more than a million Swedes would come to the United States and help build the cities and farms of the midwest.

The experiences of the earliest wave of these immigrants were captured in a series of novels by the Swedish writer Vilhelm Moberg. The excerpt comes from "A Cargo of Dreams," a chapter in the first book of the series, *The Emigrants*. It is 1850 and Karl Oskar, a poor peasant, has decided to bring his family to the United States. As he lies on his shipboard bunk, he begins to think about the journey ahead.

· · · · · · · · · · · · · · · ·

TO BEGIN

1. What is the difference between the words *immigrant* and *emigrant?* What themes can you expect to find in a book entitled *The Emigrants?*

2. *Cargo* literally refers to "the goods carried in a ship." What does the phrase "A Cargo of Dreams" mean to you?

3. Read the first two paragraphs of the excerpt. Who is the narrator of paragraph 1? Of paragraph 2?

4. Remember, this journey takes place in 1850. Using your own experiences as well as what you have learned in school and from other sources, try to anticipate what thoughts Karl Oskar has as he lies on his bunk.

You will probably come across some unfamiliar words in this excerpt from *The Emigrants*. Remember, however, that you can enjoy and understand what you read without knowing the definition of every word. Try to use the context to guess at the unfamiliar words and phrases as you read for your interest and pleasure about Karl Oskar's journey to America. Don't be overly concerned with words and phrases you don't understand; there will be a vocabulary activity after you read, respond to, and analyze the selection.

FROM

THE EMIGRANTS

VILHELM MOBERG

Sometimes during the nights the emigrants lay awake and turned in   1
their bunks, listening to each other's movements and to all the sounds
of the ship.

Karl Oskar: We are on the voyage and very little is actually the way I   2
had thought it would be. But whether it goes well or ill, I'll never regret
my step. The stupidest thing a man can do is regret something that's already done, something that cannot be changed. Perhaps I have brought
unhappiness upon us—we may have to suffer a great deal; and all is on
my shoulders. I insisted on the emigration—if it turns out badly, I can
blame only myself.

If only we can get across this ocean, and land with our health.   3

Everything I own is in this venture. With bad luck all can be lost. At   4
home they ridiculed me. They thought I had a crazy notion. This irri-
tates me, but I won't let it get under my skin. Why should other people
necessarily like what I do? Only cowardly dogs hang about lapping up
praise, waiting to have their backs scratched. I'll have to scratch my
own back. And I'll never return with my wife and children to become a
burden to my parish—whether our venture turns out happily or not.
That pleasure I won't give anyone. No; however it goes, no one at home
shall suffer because of us. There are many back there who wish me bad
luck, so I must watch my step. The home folk are envious and begrudge
each other success, wish hardship on each other; they would be
pleased if things went wrong for me.

I don't think things will begin easily for us in America. It's hard to   5
start anew. But my health is good, and if it stays with me I can work
enough to feed us. Hardship is not going to bend me; with adversity I
shall work even harder, from pure anger. I'll work, all right, as soon as I
have my land. And no one is going to cheat me—I won't put trust in the
first soft-spoken stranger I meet.

As I lie here with my money belt around my waist I like to touch it now   6
and then. It gives me a sense of security to touch it when I want to. It holds
all I have left of worldly possessions, changed into silver coin. It's all we
have to lay our new foundation; I carry that belt night and day—no one
can steal it without first killing me. Of course, all the folk here in the hold
are simple farmers, and perhaps as honest and decent as I; but I never did
trust strangers. I suppose the other farmers are also lying here with their
money belts around their bellies. But who can know for sure that there
isn't a thief on board? He wouldn't go around saying: I'm the one who
steals! And in the jostle down here we are so close to each other we can
look under each other's shirts. The way we lie packed together one could-
n't hide even a needle from the other fellow.

I have never relied on any person, except myself—and on her, of   7
course. God be praised I have such a fine woman, industrious, thrifty, and
careful of our young ones. A farmer with a wasteful, lazy, slovenly wife
never can get ahead. And she came along with me, she did as I wished.
But I'm afraid she will regret it, although she will say nothing. Perhaps she
would rather see the whole thing undone; at times I think so. If she should
begin to look back, and wish to return, what might I do then?

No. She has agreed, once and for all. She is a woman of her word,   8
she'll stick to her promise.

It's bad luck she got with child at this time—it looks as though it had   9
been planned—the very moment we left. Now she is sensitive—and I'm
afraid the sea will aggravate her further. But I shall take care of her, and
help her with the children where I can. Luckily, she too is in good
health. . . .

Life at sea is dreary and monotonous. I must cheer her, my wife. I   10
must tell her what we are going to do, once we are settled over there—a
few years from now. When the earth in America has given us abundant
crops. When I have built a big house. When the children are grown and
can help us. When Johan can go with me out into the fields. When Lill-
Marta can help her in the house. When we have a farm without a mortgage. When we won't have to worry about the mortgage interest when
we go to sleep and when we awaken. When we are independent in our
own home. When we have begun our new life. When we live cleanly
and comfortably in a house where it doesn't smell so damn bad as it
does in this stinking hole. Yes, I'll tell her everything, as I have imagined
it.

If only I could get near her; only once, at least. There ought to be a   11
change soon.

One has such foolish thoughts. No one knows what we may have to   12
go through. The old ones think that all is arranged before one is born.
Then it doesn't matter what one does—what use would there be in
labor and struggle? But I don't agree with the old ones. I think one must
put one's strength into everything, and use one's head as well as one
can. Always I have done it at home—I'll do the same over there. And I
intend never to regret it.

But our welfare and maybe our lives depend on this emigration. If   13
only we were safely across the sea. . . .

. . . .

RESPONSE AND ANALYSIS

1. Write for a few minutes in response to what you have read. Besides summarizing,
   you may want to explore your feelings and thoughts about the reading. It may be
   helpful to consider these categories:
   a. what you understood about the reading
   b. something that puzzled you in the reading
   c. something you would like to discuss with the writer or one of the characters
   d. a memory the reading evoked
   e. how you felt about the reading

2. Make a list of the thoughts that Karl Oskar relates in the piece. Compare these
   with the ones you anticipated in the previous activity.

3. What sort of man is Karl Oskar? Bring specific evidence from the text to support
   your description. How does he compare with the immigrants you know?

4. How does Karl Oskar feel about his wife? Bring specific evidence from the text to
   support your opinion.

5. Brief mention is made of Johan and Lill-Marta. Who are they? How do you know?

6. Karl Oskar looks forward to the time when he and his family "won't have to worry
   about the mortgage interest when we go to sleep and when we awaken." What is a
   mortgage? What can you learn from this passage about peasant life in Sweden?

. . . .

FURTHER EXPLORATION OF LANGUAGE AND LITERATURE:
PROVERBS

As Karl Oskar thinks about his neighbors' reactions to his trip, he recalls a Swedish
proverb: Only cowardly dogs hang about lapping up praise, waiting to have their

backs scratched. A *proverb* is a popular saying that usually expresses wisdom about life in a colorful or descriptive way. For example, one proverb in English advises, Don't cry over spilled milk—meaning that no good will come out of regretting something that has happened in the past.

1. What does Karl Oskar mean when he says, Only cowardly dogs hang about lapping up praise, waiting to have their backs scratched?

2. Students often remember proverbs from their homeland. Below is a sampling of proverbs from other countries. What do they mean to you?
   a. Birds that fly high are able to see great distances. (Korea)
   b. Like a frog in a well. (China)
   c. Rocks in the water can't know the misery of rocks in the sun. (Haiti)
   d. Cut your coat according to the cloth. (Pakistan)
   e. He who keeps company with the wolf learns to howl. (Peru)

3. Compile a list of popular proverbs in your native language. Write a translation and a brief interpretation of each.

. . . .

VOCABULARY

In the following passages, try to determine the meaning of each underlined word by its context. (You may want to choose additional words from the reading if you found the vocabulary very challenging.) Then provide a dictionary definition either in English or in your native language. Finally, read the excerpt from *The Emigrants* a second time, paying close attention to the words you have learned as well as the other points discussed in the previous activities.

1. But whether it goes well or ill, I'll never regret my step.

2. At home they ridiculed me. They thought I had a crazy notion.

3. And I'll never return with my wife and children to become a burden to my parish—whether our venture turns out happily or not.

4. The home folk are envious and begrudge each other success, wish hardship on each other; they would be pleased if things went wrong for me.

5. Hardship is not going to bend me; with adversity I shall work even harder, from pure anger.

6. And in the jostle down here we are so close to each other we can look under each other's shirts.

7. God be praised I have such a fine woman, industrious, <u>thrifty,</u> and careful of our young ones. A farmer with a wasteful, lazy, <u>slovenly</u> wife never can get ahead.

8. Life at sea is <u>dreary</u> and <u>monotonous</u>. I must cheer her, my wife.

9. But our <u>welfare</u> and maybe our lives depend on this emigration. If only we were safely across the sea. . . .

Student Essay

As one might expect, many thoughts crossed the mind of Yessenia Briceño as she flew from Nicaragua to her parents in New York City.

IN THE AIR

YESSENIA BRICEÑO

Taking a window seat on the plane, I looked back at the airline terminal. Though I had tears in my eyes, I could still see them waving goodbye: my aunt and uncle, who had raised me the last two years; and my four cousins, who had become like my brothers and sisters. We knew that we would not see each other again for a long time. Yet the sadness was mixed with joy: although I would be leaving my loved ones in Nicaragua, I was going to rejoin my parents in the United States. My mother had gone north five years before. Two years later my father had done the same. One month ago my green card had been approved. Now it was my turn. We would finally be a family again.

With the plane in the air, I looked down. I saw the shape of the land, surrounded by two oceans, the Atlantic on the east and the Pacific on the west. It looked like the maps that hung in my classroom. I saw the roads, the towns, and the agricultural areas, browns mixed with greens. I was able to identify the big lakes, Cocibolca and the Lake of Managua. I saw many other things but I couldn't identify them. I had never traveled to the eastern part of my country.

Gradually the plane rose and soon I was so high that I couldn't enjoy the beauty of seeing my homeland from above. The plane continued to rise. I started to feel butterflies in my stomach. Was I nervous or just hungry? I hadn't eaten anything the whole day. As Nicaragua faded in the distance, I tried to be strong. I said to myself, "Now I am saying goodbye, but someday you will greet me once again. I don't know when, but I will be back."

I tried to get some rest. I closed my eyes but I still saw soft white   4
clouds. I asked myself, "What is everyone doing without me?" I thought of my best friends. It was about lunchtime at school. Were they playing volleyball in the schoolyard or sitting in the shade talking about guys? I was back with them at school. "Would you like something to eat?" the stewardess asked. This brought me back to reality. Where were we? Over Central America, Mexico, the Caribbean Sea?

I looked around the plane. Some people were watching the movie   5
that was showing. Others were sleeping, reading, looking out the window, or simply chatting with their traveling companions. I was lost in thought. I noticed the stewardesses pushing a cart that fit perfectly in the aisles. Dinner was being served. When it was my turn, the pretty blond woman asked me, "Chicken or shrimp?" I understood what she was asking me because I saw what she had served to the other passengers. I wanted the *camarones* (shrimp), a real expensive treat, but I couldn't pronounce the word in English, so I settled for the chicken. I spent the rest of the trip thinking how it would be trying to live in a place where I couldn't speak the language.

The four-and-a-half-hour crossing seemed longer, but the trip was   6
coming to an end. The captain told us to buckle our safety belts to prepare for the landing. The passengers applauded as the plane came down safely. A few moments later, as I walked off the plane, I smiled when I read a big sign: Welcome to New York. Though I had tears in my eyes, I could see my parents waving at me.

. . . .

RESPONSE AND ANALYSIS

1. Think of your journey to the United States. How does it compare with this account?

2. What background information does Yessenia provide in paragraph 1?

3. There are two main *themes,* or subjects, in this essay: what happens on the plane and what Yessenia is thinking about. Make two lists with the specific details Yessenia provides for each of these themes.

4. Yessenia had trouble thinking of an appropriate *conclusion,* or ending, to her essay. After some thought, she decided to try to connect the conclusion with the *introduction,* or opening paragraph. Reread the first two sentences of the intro-

duction and then the final two sentences of the conclusion. Which phrase is repeated?

Focus on Writing: Freewriting

Many writers like to use *freewriting* as a way to generate ideas. When you freewrite, you try to write for a number of minutes about a topic without stopping. As with journal writing, you should not be concerned with spelling, grammar, punctuation, or organization. The purpose of freewriting is to try to come up with ideas; some of these you might use in your essay, others you might not. To see how freewriting can help you generate ideas, read the sample below by Zuyapa Guzmán from Mexico. Afterward you will read the essay that Zuyapa wrote using the ideas she generated by freewriting.

. . . .

SAMPLE FREEWRITING.

I had traveled before by plane once when I was a baby. We arrived   1
at the airport an hour before it was to leave. While we were waiting my
mom asked how everything was since she left us with our uncle. She
hadn't seen us for about a year. She had been in the US and was excited
about being together again. My two sisters were talking to her about
their lives. I was sitting in the corner where the telephones were. The
time came to go to the plane. I chose to sit next to the window. My sister sat beside me. The flight attendants who came to check our seat
belts spoke Spanish. The captain made an announcement in Spanish,
too. As the plane went up in the air, I closed my eyes and felt like it was
my first time being on a plane even though I traveled once before. My
stomach moved from one way to another like a washing machine. Finally we got to the sky and there I opened my eyes and the only thing I
could see outside the window was darkness and the wing of the plane
with two red lights. I could hear the noise of the engine and the wind
passing through. This made me think about what would happen if the
engines would not respond. I was worried about what would happen.
Somehow I fell asleep.

When I opened my eyes I looked around and I saw most of the pas-   2
sengers sleeping. I felt cold and I got up to take a sheet to cover myself.

Then I started thinking about my father. I hadn't seen him for 6 years. My parents were separated since I was six years old. I didn't get love from my father and that made me sad. I wished to make a family with my mother and father but I thought that it wasn't my destiny. My mother was planning to get married and make a family. I did want to have a nice family but not with somebody taking my father's place. I didn't want to accept that man as a family member. Why doesn't she marry my father again? The time came and we arrived safely at Kennedy airport. It was about 12:30. Everybody was sleeping and they got up. Well if she gets married, I thought, I have to accept it.

. . . .

DEVELOP OR OMIT?

There is an old English proverb, Don't bite off more than you can chew. Sometimes our plans are so ambitious that we cannot effectively carry them out. The same may be said for writing. It is usually better to develop one or two themes in greater detail than to try to develop all the ideas you have for an essay.

Read the revised essay Zuyapa wrote using the ideas she generated by freewriting. Notice that she has decided to focus on one or two of the ideas while omitting others.

DESTINATION: THE UNITED STATES / DESTINY: UNKNOWN
ZUYAPA GUZMÁN

At the airport in Mexico City, I looked up at the large board with the arrival and departure information. There I saw my flight: American Airlines. Flight #488. Destination: New York City. Boarding, I asked myself, "What would await me there?"   1

My mother had come to New York City one year earlier. I stayed behind in Mexico with my uncle. Now that she had gotten settled, she had come back to bring me to live with her. I was happy at the thought of being together again with my mother. However, Mom had told me that she was thinking of getting married again. This idea really scared me. It was the fear of the unknown. I looked around at the crowds of people in the terminal all preparing to go someplace.   2

A few minutes later we were inside the plane. I sat next to an Asian man. I heard the voices of the flight attendants giving instructions. As the plane took off, I closed my eyes. My stomach moved from one way to another like a washing machine. My heart began beating fast like it   3 does when I see a horror movie. When the plane finished ascending, I opened my eyes: the only thing I could see outside through the darkness was the wing of the plane with two blinking red lights. I could hear the noise of the engine and the air conditioning passing through. What would happen if the engines did not respond? Where would we land? Where would I land?

I started to think about my parents, who were separated since I was six years old. I never knew why they separated. I suppose I was too young to understand their problems. My father would only visit me once or twice a year. Not getting love from my father made me sad. I always wished to make a family of my mother and father. Many times I imagined that my father would come to see us and that he would fall in love with my mother again. Many times I wondered, if I asked my father to come and live with us again, would he come? That day on the plane I knew that this would never happen.

While she was in New York, my mother had written me some letters telling me about a sweet person who was in love with her. They were planning to get married and make a family. Still I couldn't accept somebody else taking my father's place. I wanted to have a family but not with that man. Tears of sadness began to fall down my cheeks. I knew that I would never have the family that I wished for. "Are you alright, daughter?" my mother asked. When I told her that I was afraid that the plane would crash, she laughed. "Don't worry. We'll be fine." My father would remain in Mexico. My mother and I would be in the United States.

The Asian man sitting next to me said something to me. At first I couldn't understand him because the noise from the air conditioning was so loud. I was surprised that he spoke Spanish. While we ate dinner he told me that he was a businessman from South Korea. Every week he would travel to a different part of the world. He told me that he spoke English and Italian, in addition to Spanish, and of course, Korean, his native language. My mother had fallen asleep and we passed the rest of the flight talking. I was glad to have my mind turned away from the sadness that was pressing me down. Still when he started talking about his family, I wondered if his father and mother had divorced. I never mentioned to him what I was thinking of.

When the plane landed at Kennedy Airport, I felt more afraid than ever. I knew my destination, an apartment in Brooklyn. My destiny, however, was unknown. I said goodbye to the Korean man and I walked off the plane with my mother.

. . . .

ANALYSIS

1. Look again at Zuyapa's freewriting. Make a list of the material she has developed and included in the final draft of her essay and the material she has chosen to omit.

2. Now look at how Zuyapa has organized into paragraphs the material she chose to include. Identify the main themes in each of the seven paragraphs.

3. In addition, as Zuyapa worked on her essay, she recalled an incident from the plane ride that she had not included in her freewriting: the conversation with the Korean businessman. Zuyapa felt that she had to include more about the plane ride in order to relate the passing of time on the four- or five-hour flight. If paragraph 6 had not been included, would you have wondered what else had happened on the flight? Explain.

4. A *simile* is a kind of figurative language that makes a comparison using *like* or *as*. Identify and explain the two original similes Zuyapa has used to describe how she felt as the plane took off.

Essay Writing

. . . .

GENERATING IDEAS

Freewrite about your journey from your homeland to the United States. You may want to use the categories below as a guide, but feel free to consider anything related to the topic.

a. how you traveled

b. something you did during the trip

c. something you saw

d. something you thought about

e. how you felt

f. a conversation you had

g. how you feel about the journey today

. . . .

ASSIGNMENT

Use your freewriting as the basis of an essay about your journey to the United States. Keep in mind how Zuyapa used her freewriting to help her write her essay: some ideas she chose to develop; others she chose to omit. After you have written an early draft of your essay, share it with a teacher or a friend and explore possible revisions that would make it even more successful.

3

FIRST
DAYS

. . . .

The first days in new surroundings are unusually rich in emotions and experiences. How were your first days in the United States?

READING FROM

How the García Girls Lost Their Accents

JULIA ALVAREZ

. . . .

ESTABLISHING THE CONTEXT

To this point, the readings have related the experiences of immigrants from northern Europe who came to the United States generations ago. For years, U.S. immigration laws favored those coming from Europe, the historical source of the population of the country. In 1965, however, the Immigration and Nationality Act eliminated preferential treatment on the basis of national origin. Since that time, the great majority of immigrants to the United States have come from the Caribbean, Mexico, Central and South America, and Asia.

How the García Girls Lost Their Accents by Julia Alvarez deals with one of these relatively recent groups of newcomers to the United States—the Dominicans. In the past fifteen years alone, almost half a million Dominicans have settled in the United States, primarily in New York City. Dominican Americans have become the third-largest of the Latino communities in the United States, after those from Mexico and Cuba.

Based on the author's own experiences as a woman born in the Dominican Republic and raised in the United States, the novel tells the story of four sisters uprooted from their Caribbean homeland. In the excerpt, it is 1962 and young Yolanda Garcia is sitting in her Catholic school classroom when she encounters snow for the first time.

. . . .

TO BEGIN

1. Is snow common in your homeland? How does the climate of your hometown compare with the climate of the area where you live today? Has it been difficult for you to get accustomed to the climate?

2. Use the title, *How the García Girls Lost Their Accents,* to predict what the novel might be about.

3. *Assimilation* refers to the process by which a minority culture becomes more like

the majority culture. What connection might there be between the title of the novel and the concept of assimilation?

You will probably come across some unfamiliar words in this excerpt from *How the García Girls Lost Their Accents*. Remember, however, that you can enjoy and understand what you read without knowing the definition of every word. Try to use the context to guess at the unfamiliar words and phrases as you read for your interest and pleasure about Yolanda's first encounter with snow. Don't be overly concerned with words and phrases you don't understand; there will be a vocabulary activity to do after you read, respond to, and analyze the selection.

F R O M

HOW THE GARCÍA GIRLS LOST THEIR ACCENTS

J U L I A   A L V A R E Z

Our first year in New York we rented a small apartment with a Catholic   1
school nearby, taught by the Sisters of Charity, hefty women in long black gowns and bonnets that made them look peculiar, like dolls in mourning. I liked them a lot, especially my grandmotherly fourth-grade teacher, Sister Zoe. I had a lovely name, she said, and she had me teach the whole class how to pronounce it. *Yo-lan-da.* As the only immigrant in my class, I was put in a special seat in the first row by the window, apart from the other children so that Sister Zoe could tutor me without disturbing them. Slowly, she enunciated the new words I was to repeat: *laundromat, corn flakes, subway, snow.*

Soon I picked up enough English to understand holocaust was in the   2
air. Sister Zoe explained to a wide-eyed classroom what was happening in Cuba. Russian missiles were being assembled, trained supposedly on New York City. President Kennedy, looking worried too, was on the television at home, explaining we might have to go to war against the Communists. At school, we had air-raid drills: an ominous bell would go off and we'd file into the hall, fall to the floor, cover our heads with our coats, and imagine our hair falling out, the bones in our arms going soft. At home, Mami and my sisters and I said a rosary for world peace. I heard new vocabulary: *nuclear bomb, radioactive fallout, bomb shelter.* Sister Zoe explained how it would happen. She drew a picture of a mushroom on the blackboard and dotted a flurry of chalkmarks for the dusty fallout that would kill us all.

The months grew cold, November, December. It was dark when I got   3 up in the morning, frosty when I followed my breath to school. One morning as I sat at my desk daydreaming out the window, I saw dots in the air like the ones Sister Zoe had drawn—random at first, then lots and lots. I shrieked, "Bomb! Bomb!" Sister Zoe jerked around, her full black skirt ballooning as she hurried to my side. A few girls began to cry.

But then Sister Zoe's shocked look faded. "Why, Yolanda dear, that's snow!" She laughed. "Snow." 4

"Snow," I repeated. I looked out the window warily. All my life I had heard about the white crystals that fell out of American skies in the winter. From my desk I watched the fine powder dust the sidewalk and parked cars below. Each flake was different, Sister Zoe had said, like a person, irreplaceable and beautiful. 5

. . . .

RESPONSE AND ANALYSIS

1. Write for a few minutes in response to what you have read. Besides summarizing, you may want to explore your feelings and thoughts about the reading. It may be helpful to consider these categories:

   a. what you understood about the reading

   b. something that puzzled you in the reading

   c. something you would like to discuss with the writer or one of the characters

   d. a memory the reading evoked

   e. how you felt about the reading

2. Who is the narrator of the story?

3. What sort of woman is Sister Zoe? Bring specific evidence from the text to support your description. How does she compare with the teachers you have had?

4. Sister Zoe says that each snowflake is different and "like a person, irreplaceable and beautiful." What does this mean to you? Do you agree with the sentiment? Explain.

5. Yolanda relates a number of the new words she learns in English. Some are everyday words while others relate specifically to nuclear war. List the two sets of words. Use a dictionary to provide a definition for the words you are not familiar with.

. . . .

FURTHER EXPLORATION OF LANGUAGE AND LITERATURE:
HISTORICAL REFERENCES

A great philosopher once noted, "If you don't know everything, you can't know anything." By this he meant to emphasize that all the world's knowledge is in some way connected. A case in point: the more you know about history, the better you understand literature.

Writers often use *historical references*, briefly mentioning events that have happened in history without explaining them in detail. The historical reference is assumed to be *shared knowledge*—something that the educated reader will understand—making further explanation unnecessary. The excerpt from *How the García Girls Lost Their Accents* makes a reference to the *Cuban Missile Crisis* of 1962, a significant event in the *cold war* between the United States and Cuba, an ally of the Soviet Union. Explain these two historical references. Consult an encyclopedia if you are unfamiliar with them.

. . . .

VOCABULARY

In the following passages, try to determine the meaning of each underlined word by its context. (You may want to choose additional words from the reading if you found the vocabulary very challenging.) Then provide a dictionary definition either in English or in your native language. Finally, read the excerpt from *How the García Girls Lost Their Accents* a second time, paying close attention to the words you have learned as well as the other points discussed in the previous activities.

1. Soon I picked up enough English to understand <u>holocaust</u> was in the air. Sister Zoe explained to a wide-eyed classroom what was happening in Cuba. Russian missiles were being assembled, trained supposedly on New York City.

2. At school, we had air-raid drills: an <u>ominous</u> bell would go off and we'd file into the hall, fall to the floor, cover our heads with our coats, and imagine our hair falling out, the bones in our arms going soft.

3. At home, Mami and my sisters and I said a <u>rosary</u> for world peace.

4. One morning as I sat at my desk daydreaming out the window, I saw dots in the air like the ones Sister Zoe had drawn—<u>random</u> at first, then lots and lots.

5. "Snow," I repeated. I looked out the window <u>warily</u>. All my life I had heard about the white crystals that fell out of American skies in the winter.

Student Essay

Do you recall the sadness Pedro Batista felt and the memories that came to his mind on the day he left his home in the Dominican Republic ("Leaving Home," chapter 1)? His first days in the United States, however, were exceedingly positive.

MY FIRST DAYS IN NEW YORK

PEDRO BATISTA

1   We got off the plane in New York City, my mother, my brothers and sister, and I. I couldn't believe how big and how crowded Kennedy Airport was: flights coming in from all over and people hurrying about from place to place. I had thought that I would land in an all-English-speaking city, but I soon realized that it was not so; I heard many people from different countries speaking in their native languages, not a few speaking Spanish.

2   At that point I felt happy. I was thinking about the advantages that immigrants have here in the United States. I had heard from returning Dominicans many success stories of building a better life here. I noticed many clerks, officers, and workers in the shops and restaurants of the terminal who looked as if they had come from different parts of the world, maybe even my part. That really made me feel happy.

3   My father, who had come to the United States several months earlier, was waiting for us in the airport. Unlike some of our friends, who were left behind to live with their grandparents for years, we were apart from Papi for a short time. Nevertheless, seeing his strong and handsome face, the mustache of his lips in a big smile, was wonderful. We got into his car to go to our new and totally strange home.

4   While traveling in the car, everyone was talking excitedly, and I was enjoying my first view of my new hometown. Something very strange was the wide well-paved roads, "highways," as I learned they were called. In the Dominican Republic the roads are narrow and often poorly maintained. And the cars. Big American cars traveling at high speed in the many lanes.

5   We finally arrived "home" in Brooklyn. The streets were dirtier than I had expected, and I noticed strange writing on some of the walls of the building. My father had told us about this "graffiti." The apartment, however, was freshly painted, clean, and filled with elegant furniture

and expensive appliances. Many of my relatives and friends were waiting for us. They all asked us how we felt. We just answered, "We will get used to this life."

After several days of being in New York, we planned a trip to Manhattan to see the famous tall buildings. We walked down to the subway. "A train traveling underground?" I asked myself. "How could these people build such marvelous things?" After some minutes riding we arrived in Manhattan. I was amazed: the buildings stretched into the skies. As we rode up the elevators to the top of the Empire State Building, my ears popped and my stomach turned as if I were once again on a jumbo jet. I will never forget what I saw as I looked down from the observation deck: hundreds of yellow taxis like strange bugs and thousands of people like tiny ants.

That same day back home, the sky got dark. My father said that it was going to snow. We got ready to go outside to battle the snow. We took a camera to take photos. We put on our thickest sweaters and coats but they really weren't heavy enough. Still I felt warm as I let the snow fall on my face so I could feel it completely. I ran about trying to catch the cold white snow on my tongue.

That was the happiest day of my life. I was playing with my brothers and cousins. I was with my father again. Upstairs my family was waiting in an apartment filled with things we could never have gotten back home. I was excited and optimistic about the future. I promised myself that I was going to work hard and study so that my family could be proud of me.

. . . .

RESPONSE AND ANALYSIS

1. Think of your first days in the United States. How do they compare with this account?

2. In this essay, Pedro has chosen to focus on a few specific incidents from his first days here in the United States. List these and identify the paragraph where each is related.

3. Notice that Pedro explains in the first sentence of paragraph 3 that his father—who was waiting at the airport—had come to the United States a few months earlier. Pedro has provided background information to help make his narrative clear. Would you have been confused had this information been omitted? Explain.

4. Identify and explain the two similes Pedro uses to describe the view from the top of the Empire State Building.

5. Writers often use the conclusion to sum up what has already been explored earlier in the piece. In the conclusion to his essay, Pedro notes that he was "excited and optimistic." Where in the essay have these feelings been explored?

Focus on Writing:
Direct Quotation vs. Reported Speech

As you have seen, there are two principal ways a writer can relate what people say: through direct quotation or through reported speech. For example, at the end of paragraph 5 of his essay, Pedro writes:

They all asked us how we felt. We just answered, "We will get used to this life."

Notice that whereas the question asked by Pedro's friends and family is given through reported speech (They all asked us how we felt), the answer ("We will get used to this life") is given through direct quotation. Of course, Pedro might have chosen to relate both sentences using reported speech:

They all asked us how we felt. We just told them that we would get used to the new life.

Or he might have decided to relate both sentences using direct quotation:

They all asked us, "How do you feel?" We just answered, "We will get used to this new life."

Every writer must decide when to use direct quotation and when to use reported speech. Why do you think Pedro chose to relate the conversation the way he did? Where else in the essay has Pedro related what he or others have said? Has he used direct quotation or reported speech? Explain why you believe he decided to use one or the other.

Generally, you will use more reported speech than direct quotation in your essays. However, you will usually want to provide a direct quotation or two for words or lines of particular importance. A well-placed direct quotation can add a sense of realism to your writing that will convey what you want to say more successfully.

1. Go back to the other essays you have read so far. For each, list the instances of direct quotation and reported speech. Explain why you believe the writer decided to use one or the other.

2. For further practice, revise any of the essays you have written with the aim of using direct quotation or reported speech more effectively.

Focus on Writing:
Choosing a Title

To quote an old English proverb, "Don't put the cart before the horse." In other words, do things in an appropriate order. You might spend a lot of time trying to think of a title for an essay *before* you write it. This is often difficult to do because you may not really know what you are going to write until you have written it. Certainly, you can't be expected to choose a title for your essay until you know what you are going to write. So it is often easier to choose a title *after* you've written your essay.

One more note about titles: if you can't think of a title, it may be because your essay has no real focus—you haven't written about anything meaningful. If you can't think of a title for your essay, you may want to consider doing some revision. You will find it much easier to choose an appropriate title for an essay with which you are satisfied.

At first, Genoveva Díaz from the Dominican Republic titled her essay *My First Day in the United States*. She explained quite logically that she had made the choice because that was what the assignment had been. Moreover, she maintained that the title captured what her piece was about. Upon further consideration, however, Genoveva decided that a different title would better capture the focus of her essay and arouse the reader's attention more effectively. As you read, carefully consider what the real focus is. Then try to think of an alternative title.

MY FIRST DAY IN THE UNITED STATES
(First Title)
GENOVEVA DÍAZ

"As soon as we arrive in the United States, your dad and I will take   1
you to a nice restaurant," my mom said, trying to make me feel better.
She still noticed the sadness on my face for having left *abuela*, my

grandma, behind. I didn't even try to manufacture enthusiasm. "Wake me up when we get there," was all I could say.

During the trip I was trying to get some sleep, but unfortunately I couldn't sleep for even a little while. With my eyes closed, however, I thought about how my life would be now that I would be so far away from my grandmother. Still, I was comforted by the thought that I would be reunited with my father. I thought about the past when I could see my dad only once a year. He used to come back to Santo Domingo for an entire month and spend an entire month with my mom, me, and my sisters. But what is one month out of an entire year? Now we would all be living together for good.

When we arrived, my mom said, "We're here! Wake up, Genoveva! This is the time we've been waiting for." We got off the plane and we looked for our luggage. We had neglected to put our names on our suitcases and so we had a problem locating them. Fortunately, a man who was kind and educated helped us. He also showed us the way outside to the waiting area.

We were all looking for Daddy. Suddenly my older sister, Yadira, screamed, "There he is. Come on, let's go and hug him." We all ran up to him. We were so happy at that moment. It wasn't easy for all of us to embrace, especially because he was holding heavy coats and sweaters for all of us. He explained that it was cold outside, colder than it ever was in Santo Domingo. Daddy drove us home in his big car. When we arrived we wanted to look around the street of our new home. "Just be careful," my father said, a phrase I would soon become accustomed to hearing.

My sisters decided to stay outside to look around. I wanted to go inside to call Santo Domingo to find out how my grandma was doing. She told me that she was all right and that she was relieved to hear my voice. We both said a lot of things to each other, but one part of that long and rambling conversation I will never forget. Grandma said, "I'm sure that you will find a better future there in the United States. I know it's going to be better than the one I might offer you here. I know you'll find a wonderful man who will marry you, with whom you will make a beautiful family together. You deserve it." I was overcome with emotion. "God bless you, Grandma," I said, quietly crying.

Later that night, I lay in bed listening to a Spanish-language station I had found on the radio. As I was falling asleep, I whispered, "*Te quiero, abuela.*" (I love you, Grandma.)

ANALYSIS

1. Compile a list of three or four possible alternative titles to Genoveva's essay. Then decide on one that you feel is the best. Remember, you want the title to capture the focus of the essay as well as the reader's interest.

2. The title that Genoveva ultimately chose for her essay was *"Te Quiero, Abuela"* (I love you, Grandma); she explained that after she had written the essay about her first day in the United States, she realized that thoughts of her grandmother back in the Dominican Republic dominated her emotions and experiences on that day. What is your feeling about the title Genoveva chose? In your opinion does the fact that the title is in Spanish add to or detract from its effectiveness? Explain.

3. Go back to the other student essays you have read. Focus on the titles. Are they effective? Explain.

4. For further practice, go back to the essays you have written. Revise any title that you feel could be made more effective.

Essay Writing

GENERATING IDEAS

Freewrite about your first days in the United States. You may want to use the categories below as a guide, but feel free to consider anything related to the topic.

a. your first impressions

b. something that surprised you

c. something that made you happy

d. something that made you sad

e. something you did for the first time

f. something you saw for the first time

g. a problem you faced

ASSSIGNMENT

Use your freewriting as the basis of an essay about your first days in the United States. Remember, you will not be able to include all of the material you have generated by freewriting. You must decide what to develop and what to omit. Think of a title for your essay *after* it is written, keeping in mind how Genoveva used the focus of her essay to come up with an appropriate title. Like Pedro, carefully consider when to use direct quotation or reported speech. After you have written an early draft, share it with a teacher or a friend and explore possible revisions that would make it even more successful.

4

LEARNING
ENGLISH

· · · · · · · · · · · · · · · ·

A primary concern of many newcomers to the United States is to learn and master the English language. What do you recall from the days when your English was more limited than it is today?

The Third Life of Per Smevik

O. E. RÖLVAAG

· · · · · · · · · · · · · · · ·

ESTABLISHING THE CONTEXT

You are already familiar with the work of O. E. Rölvaag from the excerpt from *The Boat of Longing* in chapter 1. All of Rölvaag's writings deal with the experiences of the Norwegian Americans who settled in the northern midwest of the United States. One historian, Theodore Blegen, would later write of Rölvaag, "With more insight and deeper power than almost any writer, he recorded and interpreted the American transition of the immigrants who made their way in the western world."

The following excerpt is from Rölvaag's first novel, *The Third Life of Per Smevik*. Like his other writings, it was originally written in Norwegian. Published in 1912, it was translated for the first time into English by his daughter and granddaughter more than a half-century later. The autobiographical novel is a series of fictional letters written by a young Norwegian immigrant to his family back home. To the young man it seems as if he has already lived two lives: the first comprising twenty-one years in Norway; the second, his month-long journey across the Atlantic and out west to his uncle's farm. His third life begins now that he has reached his destination in the United States.

· · · · · · · · · · · · · · · ·

TO BEGIN

1. Do you ever feel as if you have had two lives, one back in your homeland and one in the United States? Explain.

2. The excerpt comes from "Adjusting," the first chapter of the novel. What does the word *adjusting* mean to you? How has your adjustment to the United States been?

3. Look at the letter. Where and when was it written? Who wrote it? To whom?

You will probably come across some unfamiliar words in this excerpt from *The Third Life of Per Smevik*. Remember, however, that you can enjoy and understand what you read without knowing the definition of every word. Try to use the context to guess at the unfamiliar words and phrases as you read for your interest and pleasure the letter that Smevik has written to his brother. Don't be overly concerned with words and phrases you don't understand; there will be a vocabulary activity to do after you read, respond to, and analyze the selection.

FROM

THE THIRD LIFE OF PER SMEVIK

O. E. RÖLVAAG

Clarkfield, South Dakota
February 15, 1897

Dear Brother,

Your New Year's letter has long since been absorbed. I thank you for 1
it, although you really deserve a thrashing instead. Only four pages! What kind of a brother writes only four short pages? That's almost as good as nothing, and you will certainly have to improve. Can't you understand that I have to know about absolutely every single thing? Instead of telling me about all the fun you had at Christmas this year— about skating, the Christmas parties, and all the other things you did—you let it go with only, "There wasn't much fun this Christmas." You are just as silent about other matters. About the fishing during Advent you say only, "Both the herring and other fishing were good the whole time." News like that is worse than no news at all.

If you hadn't said anything my thoughts would have had nothing to 2
feed on and I might have been happier. I don't understand, either, how you can expect mile-long letters from me when all you write is a scant four pages. There's no justice in that.

By this time you must be at Værøy. I hope this finds you hale and 3
hearty and in the midst of some good fishing. Greet all my friends out there.

My work this winter is rather boring. I get up at half-past six, do chores 4
until half-past seven, then eat breakfast. If the weather is good, I haul a load of wheat to town, and get home again between four and five o'clock. Supper is at six, and then we go out and grub around in the manure again until eight. The rest of the evening is devoted to learning English.

I have gotten pretty good at English now, although I must admit that it goes more slowly than I had expected. It's a terribly difficult language to learn. The worst of it is, the words are spelled so differently from the way they are pronounced. You have to learn each word twice, both spelling and pronunciation, and that's not so easy. It's no wonder that the spelling is mixed-up for there are not as many letters in English as in Norwegian, neither æ, nor ø, nor å. Naturally that causes difficulty. The English word "honor," for instance, is pronounced "ahner" but it has to be spelled *honor.* Have you ever heard of anything so ridiculous? But I don't dare say anything about it or people will think I am dumb and don't understand anything.

There are other difficulties too. Many words sound very much alike, yet their meanings are as different as land and water. An experience I had last week will show you what I mean. I was in town one day and wanted to buy some writing supplies, pens among other items. I now know that writing materials are sold in drugstores in this country, which doesn't make sense to me. I went to the hardware store to buy a few things for my boss. While there it occurred to me that they sold steel and iron goods, and since pens are made of steel they might have some.

"Have you got any pents?" I asked.

"Pants?"

"Yes, pents."

"Yes."

Thereupon he took me through a side door into a clothing store which belonged to the same firm, and called to one of the clerks to show me some pants. Right then I began to suspect a mistake, but didn't let on. There was a Norwegian clerk there whom I knew slightly. Very politely he asked me in Norwegian, "What kind of trousers did you want?"

"Trousers?"

"Yes, wasn't that what you wanted?"

"Ye-es, I guess I need a pair of Sunday trousers."

But of all the dozen pairs of pants he showed me I couldn't find any I liked, and of course I did not buy any either. When I got home I looked in the dictionary and found that what we use for writing are called "pens" and the other are "pants." You can see for yourself that there is a big difference in these words as far as the spelling is concerned, but I assure you that the pronunciation is so much alike that a newcomer can scarcely hear the difference. You should have heard how my boss laughed when I told him this story!

This is certainly not the only predicament I have been in on account 16
of English. Not by a long shot. It's hard to remember some of these
words, and when I forget them I'm really in trouble. One day I was in
town and went into a store to buy a pair of suspenders; mine had broken in the morning as we were loading up. Uncle Hans told me before I
left that the English word was "suspenders." That was such a difficult
word to remember that I sat and chewed and chewed on it all the way
to town, until I was absolutely certain I would remember it. And remember it I did, right until I got inside the door. But when I got up to the
counter, ready to say what I wanted, wouldn't you know that word had
disappeared without a trace. Was I embarrassed! There I stood, with my
mouth open, staring about, unable to say a word. If it hadn't been a lady
clerk, I could have explained what I wanted with gestures, but I
couldn't possibly begin to point to the buttons on my pants to a lady,
and a young, refined lady at that. I hurried out and was so angry I
slammed the door after me. They will never see me at that store again,
you can bet on that.

The worst fix I got into on account of not remembering a word was 17
one day shortly before Christmas when I went to Clarkfield to see a doctor. That was just after I had finished the threshing run. I can't really say
I was sick exactly, just felt a little poorly. I didn't have any appetite, and
right after breakfast felt sick to my stomach. Uncle Hans thought it
might be a touch of malaria and urged me to see a doctor. Well, one
day I was feeling worse and since I was in town anyway, I decided to
throw away a dollar on one of these quacks, for of course, that's what
the doctors are in this country. I sauntered into the office of one of these
fellows who is supposed to be able to cure anything. I knew perfectly
well before I went in that the English word to use was "stomach." Isn't
that a strange word? But when I got in do you suppose I could remember it? Not on your life! He was a real grouch, and I suppose I got a little
flustered, so I forgot. At any rate this blamed "stomach" had disappeared from my memory.

There I stood, making faces and trying to look sick, while I tried to 18
explain in English that I had a pain below my chest, a long way below
my chest. And he began to growl and scold and question me, but it all
went so furiously fast that I couldn't follow. Besides he looked so angry
that I was on the point of running out. But then I got angry too. Here I
had been in America four months and I still couldn't manage to explain
such a simple thing as being sick to my stomach. Well, I thought, if I

can't use words, I will just have to get along with gestures. So I began to pat my stomach, then I opened my mouth wide and stuck my hand so far into my throat that the tears came, all the while stammering, "In the morning, in the morning." Well, that helped. The old sourpuss had to laugh at last, although I couldn't see what was so funny myself. Then he sat down and wrote a prescription for me. For this he charged me a whole dollar. Yes sir, one whole dollar. Then he told me to go to the drugstore and get the medicine.

When I came out on the street again I began to consider this, and   19
came to the conclusion that I had better be careful. Suppose that old grouch of a doctor had misunderstood me, though I thought I had explained very clearly, and given me a medicine for some sickness I didn't have at all? Guess what I did then. I stuffed that prescription into my pocket and drove home. I told Uncle Hans that I had seen the doctor but that he hadn't given me any medicine, which was true. I should just eat eggs for breakfast, he'd said. "Well," answered Uncle Hans, "if you don't need anything more than eggs for breakfast, I'll see that you soon get well." Since then I have lived like a king on eggs. Now I'm almost tired of them, and my stomach is certainly not any worse. So now you see the many trials and tribulations of learning English.

I can't write any more this time. Please be a real good fellow and   20
write me a long letter. You must tell me everything from Værøy, about the fishing and everything else. Is there night school this year? Who is the teacher? If it's the same one as last year, you must greet him from me. Have they gotten any new books in the fisherman's library?

Remember to write about everything.   21

Your affectionate brother,
P. A. Smevik

. . . .

RESPONSE AND ANALYSIS

1. Write for a few minutes in response to what you have read. Besides summarizing, you may want to explore your feelings and thoughts about the reading. It may be helpful to consider these categories:

   a. what you understood about the reading

   b. something that puzzled you in the reading

   c. something you would like to discuss with the writer or one of the characters

   d. a memory the reading evoked

   e. how you felt about the reading

2. What is Smevik's complaint in the first paragraph?

3. Smevik mentions several qualities of English that he finds troublesome. List these.

4. To illustrate his difficulties with learning English, Smevik relates a number of anecdotes. Briefly summarize these.

5. How do your experiences compare with those of Smevik?

. . . .

FURTHER EXPLORATION OF LANGUAGE AND LITERATURE: ENGLISH SPELLING

Smevik observes of English that "the words are spelled . . . differently from the way they are pronounced." English spelling is highly irregular—often there is no one-to-one correspondence between letter and sound. One letter may represent different sounds. This is especially true of the letters used for vowel sounds.

The Irish writer George Bernard Shaw noted that English spelling is so irregular that it is possible to pronounce the spelling *ghoti* as "fish." How? In the word *enough,* for example, the *gh* is pronounced *f.* The *o* in the word *women* is pronounced like a short *i.* And the *ti* in a word such as *nation* is pronounced like *sh.*

Nevertheless, attempts to reform English spelling to make it more regular have failed. Such reform would involve reprinting all books in the new spelling and requiring that students learn to decode in both the old system and the new one.

One student noted that she was forever confusing the spelling of the words *though, through,* and *thought,* no matter how many times she checked for the correct spelling in a dictionary. Make a list of words in English whose spelling has been particularly troubling for you. This time, make sure you spell them correctly!

. . . .

VOCABULARY

In the following passages, try to determine the meaning of each underlined word by its context. (You may want to choose additional words from the reading if you found the vocabulary very challenging.) Then provide a dictionary definition either in English or in your native language. Finally, read the excerpt from *The Third Life of Per Smevik* a second time, paying close attention to the words you have learned as well as the other points discussed in the previous activities.

1. I thank you for it, although you really deserve a <u>thrashing</u> instead. Only four pages!

2. I get up at half-past six, do <u>chores</u> until half-past seven, then eat breakfast.

3. While there it occurred to me that they sold steel and iron <u>goods</u>, and since pens are made of steel they might have some.

4. There was a Norwegian clerk there whom I knew <u>slightly.</u>

5. This is certainly not the only <u>predicament</u> I have been in on account of English.

6. I <u>sauntered</u> into the office of one of these fellows who is supposed to be able to cure anything.

7. So I began to pat my stomach, then I opened my mouth wide and stuck my hand so far into my throat that the tears came, all the while <u>stammering,</u> "In the morning, in the morning."

8. So now you see the many <u>trials and tribulations</u> of learning English.

Student Essay

Were you ever in an uncomfortable situation because you were unable to understand or speak the language of your surroundings? Joel Hernández recalls the year he came from Puerto Rico and began to attend school on the mainland of the United States. His limited English led to a misunderstanding and this painful memory.

A PAINFUL MEMORY

JOEL HERNÁNDEZ

For most immigrants it is very difficult to learn English. There is al-   1
ways a time where the immigrant with limited English becomes involved in a problem because of his inability to understand the language
or communicate satisfactorily. I can still remember some years ago
when I first came to the United States. I can't say that I didn't know a
word of English, but I didn't know much more.

It was 1985 when I first came to New York City. For me it was a   2
dream come true—making it to the Land of Unlimited Opportunities.
Unforgettable experiences awaited, not all of them positive, as it would
turn out. Even during those first moments here I was already imagining
how I might be humiliated because I knew little English.

I would start a new school, a huge brick building on Bushwick Av-   3
enue. In my mind I was saying, "How am I going to communicate with
my teachers?" I wasn't so worried about the students because I felt that I
would find someone who could speak Spanish.

I was so relieved to find that the school had a bilingual program with   4 many teachers who spoke my language. Even my art teacher spoke enough Spanish so we could communicate with each other. That was my favorite class; I began to show my natural ability to draw. I received a certificate for my art projects and my mastery of technique. This was the first academic award I had ever received.

However, not all went so well. One day, my English teacher, who   5
could speak some Spanish, took the class to the computer room to teach us how to use a word processor. After a few moments, I saw the teacher get ready to leave. I began to be nervous: would the computer teacher speak Spanish?

There I was: though there was a room full of students, I felt alone. I   6
noticed a man whom I had never seen before walking towards my desk. Apparently, he was the computer teacher. My heart began to pound and I nervously started cracking my knuckles. The teacher stopped beside me. "Press the lower right button and then at the same time press the shift key," he told me. I tried to follow what he had said but I didn't press both keys simultaneously. So he repeated the instructions, but again I pressed one key, released it, and then the other. He started to raise his voice. "Leave the key down while you press the other one, young man." I told him in Spanish, "*Yo no entiendo lo que usted está diciendo.*" (I don't understand what you are saying.)

Finally the teacher asked a student sitting next to me what I had just   7
said. The girl explained. The teacher responded, "Why didn't he say something in the first place?" Obviously, I couldn't . . . I couldn't say what I wanted to in English. The teacher apologized but I thought: "Now he says he's sorry after embarrassing me in front of all the students."

I will never forget that day when the teacher screamed at me in pub-   8
lic. I wish I could say that was the only problem I encountered due to my limited English, but like so many other immigrants, I could probably write a book.

. . . .

RESPONSE AND ANALYSIS

1. The introductory paragraph often provides the reader with an idea of what the essay will be about. Does Joel's introduction accomplish this? Explain.

2. In paragraph 4, Joel relates a number of positive experiences. List these. Keeping in mind that the main point of the essay is the humiliating experience he had in the computer room, do you feel that paragraph 4 adds to or detracts from the essay? Explain.

3. *Transitions* are connections between sentences or paragraphs. Explain how the first sentence in paragraph 5—"However, not all went so well . . . "—connects paragraph 4 with paragraph 5.

4. What two phrases does Joel use to convey his nervousness when his regular teacher leaves the room?

5. Like the title that Genoveva Díaz ultimately chose for her essay in the previous chapter, Joel relates his response to the teacher in paragraph 6 in Spanish, providing the English translation in parentheses. Why do you think he chose to tell the story this way? Does this technique add to or detract from the essay?

Focus on Writing: The Introduction

When students write an in-class essay, it is not uncommon to see them struggling with the opening paragraph. The introduction, like the title, is often difficult to write first because most of us are not really certain what we want to write until we actually write it. It often helps to write the introduction after you write the *body,* or the part where the main theme of the essay is developed. Let's explore two techniques that will help you find an elegant way to begin your essay.

. . . .

MOVE FROM THE GENERAL TO THE SPECIFIC

You probably have heard many times that a good introduction should give the reader an idea of what the essay will be about. Notice that Joel begins his essay with a *general* statement about immigrants with limited English. He then moves on to the *specific* details of his anecdote.

. . . .

MOVE FROM THE SPECIFIC TO THE GENERAL

Genoveva Díaz took a different approach in writing the opening paragraph to her essay, *"Te Quiero, Abuela"* (initially titled, "My First Day in The United States"), in the previous chapter. Notice how Genoveva begins with a direct quotation, catching the attention of her readers with a specific detail of the narrative: "As soon as we arrive in the United States, your Dad and I will take you to a nice restaurant." Only afterward, in the second paragraph, does she provide the appropriate "introductory" material, explaining that she had just left her grandmother in Santo Domingo to be reunited with her father.

To get a better idea about these two approaches toward writing an introduction, read the two versions of an essay written by Andrzej Sas from Poland about a misunderstanding he had with an auto mechanic. Andy was not entirely satisfied with the early draft. Instead of changing the content of the essay, Andy rewrote the introduction and reorganized the material.

ANXIOUS WITH ENGLISH

(Early Draft)

ANDRZEJ SAS

Everyone feels anxious sometimes, even a quiet and calm man like 1 myself. One incident which caused me great anxiety happened a few years ago when my English was more limited than it is today. I had been in the United States for a little more than a year at the time. If somebody asked me about my English, I answered, "Give me a break. I can start to learn English later. First I must work and save money." At least that was what I tried to say in English. I might have made some mistakes!

One day I had some problems with my car. I decided to go to the 2 auto mechanic myself. I only wanted to have the oil changed and the spark plugs replaced. I thought that I knew enough English to order that service. It should have cost about $50. I also knew that in about a month or two, I would have to replace my front brakes so I asked the mechanic about the price for that job. I left the car and then went to the dentist.

When I came back in a couple of hours and asked about the bill, 3 there was an unpleasant surprise. The mechanic had not understood me correctly and he had done the brake job. The bill came to more than $200. I was very upset. I had only $50. I tried to explain the problem but I couldn't because my English was not good enough. At that time I had a lot of expenses. I had my dental bills to take care of. Also, it was the end of the month so I had to pay the rent as well as the phone bill. I didn't know what to do. I decided to call my boss and ask for help. Fortunately, he was a generous man and he helped me out of my trouble.

After that occurrence, I understood that money is not the most impor- 4 tant thing in life. In order to live in the United States I should start to study immediately, intensively, and seriously. So I have!

As you read the final version of the essay, note the difference in the introduction. Afterward you will be able to analyze why Andy decided to make the revision.

ANXIOUS WITH ENGLISH

(Revised Essay)

ANDRZEJ SAS

"That'll be $200," the mechanic told me when I came to pick up my   1
car. I thought I had not heard him correctly. An oil change and new
spark plugs should cost about $50. With a sick feeling in my stomach I
started to put together what had happened. When I dropped off my car
a few hours before, I had asked how much it would be to have new
front brakes installed. I knew that the brakes were going and in about a
month or two I would have to replace them. I realized that I had not
made myself clear. The mechanic had installed new brakes. I had only
wanted to inquire about the price.

I had been in the United States for a little more than a year at the   2
time. If somebody asked me about my English, I answered, "Give me a
break. I can start to learn English later. First I must work and save
money." At least that's what I tried to say. I might have made some mistakes. At that point in my life it was more important to work and earn as
much money as I could than to go to night school to study English.

I tried to explain the problem to the mechanic but I couldn't because   3
my English was not good enough. At that time I had a lot of expenses. I
had my dental bills to take care of. Also, it was at the end of the month
so I had to pay the rent as well as the phone bill. I didn't know what to
do. I decided to call my boss and ask for help. Fortunately, he was a
generous man and he helped me out of my trouble.

After that occurrence, I understood that money is not the most impor-   4
tant thing in life. In order to live in the United States I should start to
study English immediately, intensively, and seriously. So I have!

. . . .

ANALYSIS

1. Notice that in the introduction of his early draft Andrzej begins with a general
   statement: "Everyone feels anxious sometimes. . . . " Then he provides some appropriate background information when he mentions that he had been in the
   United States for a little more than a year at the time. In his revision, Andrzej decided to change the introduction. Instead of starting his essay with a general
   statement and background information, he decided to start with a direct quotation from the anecdote he was relating. Not until the second paragraph does he

provide the background information. Which version of the essay do you prefer? Why?

2. Go back to the other student essays you have read. Focus on the introductions. Do the essays move from general to specific or from specific to general?

3. Another technique you might consider using as you write your introduction is to start with a *rhetorical question*—a question to which you don't really expect an answer, but ask in order to raise an issue. One student—Jean Pierrelouis from Haiti—began an essay with this rhetorical question:

Do you realize how difficult it is to come to the United States without knowing English well?

He then proceeded to describe his attempt at ordering chicken wings in a Chinese restaurant. Having forgotten the English word for "chicken" and never knowing the one for "wings," the resourceful young man used gestures to indicate what he wanted to order.

So as Jean continued his narrative, he provided an answer to his introductory rhetorical question.

4. For further practice, go back to the essays you have written. Revise any introduction that you feel could be made more effective.

Essay Writing

. . . .

GENERATING IDEAS

You probably have a story to tell from the days when you first came to the United States and your English was not as strong as it is today. Think about such a time and make notes as you come up with ideas. Use the questions below as a guide, but feel free to consider anything related to the topic.

a. Where and when did the incident happen?

b. How long had you been in the United States?

c. Who was involved?

d. What happened?

e. What were the results of your inability to communicate effectively?

f. How did you feel?

g. What, if anything, did you learn from the experience?

h. Looking back, how do you feel about the incident now?

. . . .

ASSIGNMENT

Use the ideas you generated in the previous activity as the basis of an essay about an incident you were involved in because of your limited English. If you have trouble starting, go directly into the narrative. Afterward, you can provide the necessary "introductory" material, such as the background information or a general statement about the problems of the immigrant from a non-English-speaking country. After you have written an early draft of your essay, share it with a teacher or a friend and explore possible revisions that would make it even more successful.

5

CULTURE

· · · · · · · · · · · · · · · · ·

Because many immigrants find life in their new home so different from that in their native land, they often go through a period of adjustment called *culture shock*. What differences have you noticed between ways of life in the United States and in your homeland?

R E A D I N G   F R O M

In the Year of the Boar and Jackie Robinson
B E T T E   B A O   L O R D

· · · · · · · · · · · · · · · ·

ESTABLISHING THE CONTEXT

The Chinese began to come in substantial numbers to the United States with the discovery of gold in California in 1849. Some years later Chinese laborers would work with Irish immigrants to build the transcontinental railroad linking the east and west coasts of the country. However, as the Chinese became a more significant component of the population and labor force, discriminatory measures were enacted to restrict their entry. The Chinese Exclusion Act of 1882, in fact, signaled the end of free immigration to the United States.

The twentieth century has seen periods of greater or lesser immigration from China; the numbers are influenced by world events and American immigration policy. The elimination of the quota system based on national origins has resulted in a dramatic increase in Chinese immigration in recent years.

Bette Bao Lord's *In the Year of the Boar and Jackie Robinson* takes place in Brooklyn, New York, in 1947. Like many of the other readings, the novel was based on the author's experiences as a newcomer to the United States. The excerpt finds Shirley Temple Wong, who has just arrived from China, in the process of registering for school.

· · · · · · · · · · · · · · · ·

TO BEGIN

1. The title of the novel, *In the Year of the Boar and Jackie Robinson*, makes two *cultural references*—references to familiar terms that the author assumes the educated reader will understand. Use an encyclopedia to investigate these references if they are unfamiliar to you. You should find a separate entry for Jackie Robinson, a great American hero. To understand the phrase "The Year of the Boar," you will probably have to look under *calendars* or *Chinese calendar*.

2. Some students have suggested that by *juxtaposing* (placing side by side) the two phrases "The Year of the Boar" and "Jackie Robinson," the author hoped to introduce the idea of assimilation. What does this observation mean to you?

3. Read paragraph 1 of the selection. Can you relate to the way Shirley is feeling? What was your first day of school like in the United States? Explain.

4. Read the last paragraph. Shirley's father, reading from a note sent by her teacher, says, "Your teacher suggests we take you to a doctor. She thinks there is something wrong with your eyes." After you complete the reading, be prepared to explain why the teacher believes that there is something wrong with Shirley's eyes.

You will probably come across some unfamiliar words in this excerpt from *In the Year of the Boar and Jackie Robinson*. Remember, however, that you can enjoy and understand what you read without knowing the definition of every word. Try to use the context to guess at the unfamiliar words and phrases as you read for your interest and pleasure about Shirley's first day at school. Don't be overly concerned with words and phrases you don't understand; there will be a vocabulary activity to do after you read, respond to, and analyze the selection.

FROM

IN THE YEAR OF THE BOAR AND JACKIE ROBINSON

BETTE BAO LORD

Nine o'clock sharp the very next morning, Shirley sat in the principal's 1
office at P. S. 8. Her mother and the schoolmistress were talking. Shirley
didn't understand a word. It was embarrassing. Why hadn't she, too,
studied the English course on the records that Father had sent? But it
was too late now. She stopped trying to understand. Suddenly, Mother
hissed, in Chinese, "Stop that or else!"

Shirley snapped her head down. She had been staring at the stranger. 2
But she could not keep her eyes from rolling up again. There was something
more foreign about the principal than about any other foreigner she
had seen so far. What was it? It was not the blue eyes. Many others had
them too. It was not the high nose. All foreign noses were higher than Chinese
ones. It was not the blue hair. Hair came in all colors in America.

Yes, of course, naturally. The woman had no eyelashes. Other for- 3
eigners grew hair all over them, more than six Chinese together. This
woman had none. Her skin was as bare as the Happy Buddha's belly,
except for the neat rows of stiff curls that hugged her head.

She had no eyebrows, even. They were penciled on, and looked just   4
like the character for man, 人. And every time she tilted her head, her
hair moved all in one piece like a hat.

"Shirley."   5

Mother was trying to get her attention. "Tell the principal how old   6
you are."

Shirley put up ten fingers.   7

While the principal filled out a form, mother argued excitedly. But   8
why? Shirley had given the correct answer. She counted just to make
sure. On the day she was born, she was one year old. And two months
later, upon the new year, she was two. That was the Year of the Rabbit.
Then came the Dragon, Snake, Horse, Sheep, Monkey, Rooster,
Dog and now it was the year of the Boar, making ten. Proof she was
ten.

Mother shook her head. Apparently, she had lost the argument. She   9
announced in Chinese, "Shirley, you will enter fifth grade."

"Fifth? But, Mother, I don't speak English. And besides, I only com-   10
pleted three grades in Chungking."

"I know. But the principal has explained that in America everyone is   11
assigned according to age. Ten years old means fifth grade. And we
must observe the American rules, mustn't we?"

Shirley nodded obediently. But she could not help thinking that only   12
Shirley had to go to school, and only Shirley would be in trouble if she
failed.

Mother stood up to leave. She took Shirley by the hand. "Remember,   13
my daughter, you may be the only Chinese these Americans will ever
meet. Do your best. Be extra good. Upon your shoulders rests the reputation of all Chinese."

All five hundred million? Shirley wondered.   14

"You are China's little ambassador."   15

"Yes, Mother." Shirley squared her shoulders and tried to feel worthy   16
of this great honor. At the same time she wished she could leave with
Mother.

Alone, the schoolmistress and Shirley looked at each other. Suddenly   17
the principal shut one eye, the right one, then opened it again.

Was this another foreign custom, like shaking hands? It must be   18
proper if a principal does it, Shirley thought. She ought to return the ges-
ture, but she didn't know how. So she shut and opened both eyes.
Twice.

This brought a warm laugh.   19

The principal then led her to class. The room was large, with win-   20
dows up to the ceiling. Row after row of students, each one unlike the
next. Some faces were white, like clean plates; others black like ebony.
Some were in-between shades. A few were spotted all over. One boy
was as big around as a water jar. Several others were as thin as chopsticks. No one wore a uniform of blue, like hers. There were sweaters
with animals on them, shirts with stripes and shirts with squares, dresses
in colors as varied as Grand-grand Uncle's paints. Three girls even wore
earrings.

While Shirley looked about, the principal had been making a   21
speech. Suddenly it ended with "Shirley Temple Wong." The class
stood up and waved.

Amitabha! They were all so tall. Even Water Jar was a head taller   22
than she. For a fleeting moment she wondered if Mother would consider buying an ambassador a pair of high-heeled shoes.

"Hi, Shirley!" The class shouted.   23

Shirley bowed deeply. Then, taking a guess, she replied, "Hi!"   24

The teacher introduced herself and showed the new pupil to a front-   25
row seat. Shirley liked her right away, although she had a most difficult
name, Mrs. Rappaport. She was a tiny woman with dainty bones and
fiery red hair brushed skyward. Shirley thought that in her previous life
she must have been a bird, a cardinal perhaps. Yet she commanded respect, for no student talked out of turn. Or was it the long mean pole
that hung on the wall behind the desk that commanded respect? It
dwarfed the bamboo cane the teacher in Chungking had used to punish
Four Hands whenever he stole a trifle from another.

Throughout the lessons, Shirley leaned forward, barely touching her   26
seat, to catch the meaning, but the words sounded like gurgling water.
Now and then, when Mrs. Rappaport looked her way, she opened and
shut her eyes as the principal had done, to show friendship.

At lunchtime, Shirley went with the class to the school cafeteria, but   27
before she could pick up a tray, several boys and girls waved for her to
follow them. They were smiling, so she went along. They snuck back to
the classroom to pick up coats, then hurried out the door and across the
school yard to a nearby store. Shirley was certain they should not be
there, but what choice did she have? These were now her friends.

One by one they gave their lunch money to the store owner, whom   28
they called "Mr. P." In return, he gave each a bottle of orange-colored

water, bread twice the size of an ear of corn oozing with meat balls, peppers, onions, and hot red gravy, and a large piece of brown paper to lay on the icy sidewalk and sit upon. While they ate, everyone except Shirley played marbles or cards and traded bottle caps and pictures of men swinging a stick or wearing one huge glove. It was the best lunch Shirley had ever had.

And there was more. After lunch, each of them was allowed to select   29
one item from those displayed under the glass counter. There were paper strips dotted with red and yellow sugar tacks, chocolate soldiers in blue tin foil, boxes of raisins and nuts, envelopes of chips, cookies as big as pancakes, candy elephants, lollipops in every color, a wax collection of red lips, white teeth, pink ears and curly black mustaches. Shirley was the last to make up her mind. She chose a hand, filled with juice. It looked better than it tasted, but she did not mind. Tomorrow she could choose again.

But when she was back in her seat, waiting for Mrs. Rappaport to   30
enter the classroom, Shirley's knees shook. What if the teacher found out about her escapade? There would go her ambassadorship. She would be shamed. Her parents would lose face. All five hundred million Chinese would suffer. Round and round in her stomach the meat balls tumbled like pebbles.

Then Mrs. Rappaport came in. She did not look pleased. Shirley   31
flinched when the teacher went straight to the long mean pole. For the first time her heart went out to Four Hands. She shut her eyes and prayed to the Goddess of Mercy. Oh Kwan Yin, please don't let me cry! She waited, listening for Mrs. Rappaport's footsteps to become louder and louder. They did not. Finally curiosity overcame fear and she looked up. Mrs. Rappaport was using the pole to open a window!

The lessons continued. During arithmetic, Shirley raised her hand.   32
She went to the blackboard and wrote the correct answer. Mrs. Rappaport rewarded her with a big smile. Shirley opened and shut her eyes to show her pleasure. Soon, she was dreaming about candy elephants and cookies the size of pancakes.

Then school was over. As Shirley was putting on her coat, Mrs. Rap-   33
paport handed her a letter, obviously to be given to her parents. Fear returned. Round and round, this time like rocks.

She barely greeted her mother at the door.   34

"What happened?"   35

"Nothing."   36

"You look sick."   37

"I'm all right."   38

"Perhaps it was something you ate at lunch?"   •   39

"No," she said much too quickly. "Nothing at all to do with lunch."   40

"What then?"   41

"The job of ambassador is harder than I thought."   42

At bedtime, Shirley could no longer put off giving up the letter. Trem-   43
bling, she handed it to Father. She imagined herself on a boat back to
China.

He read it aloud to Mother. Then they both turned to her, a most   44
quizzical look on their faces.

"Your teacher suggests we take you to a doctor. She thinks there is   45
something wrong with your eyes."

. . . .

RESPONSE AND ANALYSIS

1. Write for a few minutes in response to what you have read. Besides summarizing,
   you may want to explore your feelings and thoughts about the reading. It may be
   helpful to consider these categories:

   a. what you understood about the reading

   b. something that puzzled you in the reading

   c. something you would like to discuss with the writer or one of the characters

   d. a memory the reading evoked

   e. how you felt about the reading

2. Explain why Mrs. Rappaport believed that Shirley might need glasses.

3. Another misunderstanding involves the wooden pole used to open windows. At
   first, what did Shirley believe was the function of the pole?

4. Shirley's mother tells her, "Upon your shoulders rests the reputation of all Chinese." What did the mother mean by this? In your opinion, was it fair of the
   mother to give her daughter this responsibility? Explain.

5. Locate the part of the story where Shirley refers to the Chinese calendar. Why is it
   mentioned at this point?

6. Two other subtle cultural references are made in the excerpt. One is a reference

to baseball cards, the other to *reincarnation,* the belief that after death the soul returns to life in a new body. Locate these references.

7. Throughout the story, Shirley notes a number of the differences between China and the United States. Discuss these.

....

FURTHER EXPLORATION OF LANGUAGE AND LITERATURE: SIMILES

You may recall the similes that Zuyapa Guzmán used in her essay in chapter 2 to describe her nervousness on the flight from Mexico to the United States:

My stomach moved from one way to another like a washing machine. My heart began beating fast like it does when I see a horror movie.

Or those used by Pedro Batista in his essay in chapter 3 to describe the view from the top of the Empire State Building:

I will never forget what I saw as I looked down from the observation deck: hundreds of yellow taxis like strange bugs and thousands of people like tiny ants.

As you've seen, a simile is a type of figurative language that makes a comparison using the words *like* or *as.* It is perhaps the most basic kind of figurative language and has been used for thousands of years in many different parts of the world. The excerpt from *In the Year of the Boar and Jackie Robinson* contains a number of similes. When Shirley looks around at her new classmates she notices that some are "white, like clean plates." One boy is "big around as a water jar." Others are "as thin as chopsticks."

1. Identify the other similes used in the excerpt.

2. Compile a list of some similes you are familiar with, either in English or in your native language (in translation, of course!).

....

VOCABULARY

In the following passages, try to determine the meaning of each underlined word by its context. (You may want to choose additional words from the reading if you found the vocabulary very challenging.) Then provide a dictionary definition either in English or in your native language. Finally, read the excerpt from *In the Year of the*

Boar and Jackie Robinson a second time, paying close attention to the words you have learned as well as the other points discussed in the previous activities.

1. Suddenly, Mother <u>hissed,</u> in Chinese, "Stop that or else!"

2. And every time she <u>tilted</u> her head, her hair moved all in one piece like a hat.

3. For a <u>fleeting</u> moment she wondered if Mother would consider buying an ambassador a pair of high-heeled shoes.

4. Or was it the long mean pole that hung on the wall behind the desk that commanded respect? It <u>dwarfed</u> the bamboo cane the teacher in Chungking had used to punish Four Hands whenever he stole a <u>trifle</u> from another.

5. Then Mrs. Rappaport came in. She did not look pleased. Shirley <u>flinched</u> when the teacher went straight to the long mean pole.

6. At bedtime, Shirley could no longer put off giving up the letter. <u>Trembling,</u> she handed it to Father. She imagined herself on a boat back to China.

Student Essay

In his essay, Lei Zhang from China identifies two differences between the social rules of his country and those of the United States.

WHEN IN ROME

LEI ZHANG

As a Chinese man living here in the United States, I have noticed a 1 number of differences between the codes of conduct of the two countries. These differences may create misunderstandings. Therefore, I believe that it is very important for foreigners to understand the customs of Americans when they come to stay in this country.

For example, compared to the Chinese, Americans are very direct 2 people. They say what is on their minds. Not so with the Chinese. Suppose I arrive at a friend's house and he offers me something to drink. According to the customs of my people, even if I am thirsty, I must still say something such as, "No, please don't trouble yourself." My friend understands that according to our social rules, he should continue to ask me repeatedly until I concede to accept a drink. In this situation, an American guest, asked if he would like something to drink, would not hesitate to answer affirmatively. And an American host would not ask me again and again or try to press me after I have told him that I do not wish any refreshments. In fact, if I say, "No, thank you" when I really do want something to drink, I will probably find myself quite thirsty during my visit.

I think it is fair to say that as a rule, Chinese people tend to be shy   3
and modest. Excess modesty is considered to be a great virtue. When Chinese scientists arrive here to work on research, many end up working as laboratory technicians washing test tubes instead of doing the higher-level work they are fully capable of doing. They are so reserved about their abilities and knowledge, the American scholars simply are not aware of the intellectual quality of their Chinese counterparts. As a result, the Chinese are often relegated to do the less important tasks.

There is an English proverb: When in Rome, do as the Romans. Per   4
haps we Chinese should accept the local customs in order to survive and prosper here in the United States.

. . . .

RESPONSE AND ANALYSIS

1. Explain the title of the essay.

2. Of the many differences between the two peoples, Lei focuses on only two. Which?

3. In the introduction, Lei says that "it is very important for foreigners to understand the customs of Americans when they come to stay in this country." If not, unintentional misunderstandings may arise. Have you ever been involved in a situation like this? Explain.

4. In his conclusion, Lei says that Chinese people should accept American customs. Do you agree with this? Explain.

Focus on Writing: Organizing Ideas

You've seen the importance of generating ideas as an initial step in the writing process. In conjunction with this, you must also decide how to organize and develop your ideas. Drafting a *thesis statement,* including a *topic sentence* and *supporting evidence* in the paragraphs you write, and preparing an *outline* are techniques that can help you to develop and organize your material into a successful essay.

. . . .

THE THESIS STATEMENT

The *thesis* of an essay is its main idea. In a narrative essay, which tells a story, or a descriptive essay about people and places, the thesis may be *implicit* or suggested rather than stated directly. An essay where the writer takes a position and tries to prove a point, however, will usually include an *explicit* or direct statement of the main idea. The thesis statement is most often found in the introduction.

For example, notice how Lei begins with his thesis statement: "As a Chinese man living here in the United States, I have noticed a number of differences between the codes of conduct of the two countries. These differences may create misunderstandings." This main idea is developed in the other paragraphs of the essay.

. . . .

THE TOPIC SENTENCE/SUPPORTING MATERIAL

After you introduce the main idea, you will want to develop it in the other paragraphs of the essay. As the thesis statement states the main idea of an essay, the *topic sentence* states the main idea of a paragraph. Although the topic sentence usually comes at the beginning of the paragraph, sometimes you might prefer to place it in the middle or at the end.

Go back to paragraph 2 in Lei's essay. It begins with the topic sentence: "For example, compared to the Chinese, Americans are very direct people." This sentence tells in a *general* way what the paragraph is about. After he has stated the main idea of the paragraph in general terms, Lei goes on to provide some *specific* supporting material—an example about the differences between the two cultures regarding the rules of politeness when offering and accepting a beverage.

Lei has organized his ideas in paragraph 3 in a similar manner. Where does he state the main idea? What supporting evidence does he provide?

. . . .

ANECDOTAL EVIDENCE

At some point in the future, you will probably be required to do research in order to find material outside of your own personal experiences, a topic covered in chapters 11 and 12. To this point, however, your writing has been concentrated on what you have experienced, seen, or heard yourself.

We all make generalizations based on *anecdotal evidence,* that is, evidence from our own experiences and observations. For example, if I live in a community where many immigrants from Haiti have settled, I might conclude that Haitian immigrants are coming to the United States in large numbers and settling throughout the country. This may or may not be the case. Your neighborhood may indeed be typical of the rest of the country, and so your generalization—based on anecdotal evidence—may be justified. However, your neighborhood might be very atypical, making your generalization unsound. So be careful about making broad generalizations based exclusively on anecdotal evidence!

. . . .

Outlining

An *outline* is a short plan of the contents and organization of your essay. Many writers find that preparing an outline helps them to organize and develop their ideas. Look at the following outline Lei used to help him write his essay.

WHEN IN ROME
(Outline)

LEI ZHANG

Paragraph 1: Introduction
Thesis Statement: I have noticed a number of differences between the codes of conduct of the United States and China. These differences may create misunderstandings.

Paragraph 2
Topic Sentence: Americans are very direct people.
Supporting Material: Anecdote about offering refreshments to a guest.

Paragraph 3
Topic Sentence: Chinese people tend to be shy and modest.
Supporting Material: Example about Chinese scientists in the United States.

Paragraph 4
Conclusion: Chinese should accept the customs of the United States.

Based on this short outline, Lei was able to write a full-length essay.

Go back to other student essays you have read. Focus on the organization. Try to reconstruct the outlines the writers may have prepared by identifying the main idea of each paragraph and the topic sentence if one is used.

. . . .
DEVELOPING IDEAS: FROM SPECIFIC OBSERVATION
TO GENERALIZATION

The following paragraphs explore a number of the cultural differences between the United States and the student writer's homeland. Try to write a sentence that captures the main idea of each paragraph. This will approximate the thinking process: first we make specific observations; then we make generalizations based on the specifics we have noted.

Example

Once I was in a clothing store standing in line to pay for my purchase. Suddenly I noticed a man trying to take my money from my pocket. I got the attention of the store's security officer, who came and held the man until the police came. The police asked the other customers what had happened. Would you believe that not one person offered any account to the police? This could never have happened in Puerto Rico.

Main Idea: Americans are reluctant to become involved in the affairs of others.

a. I remember once I wanted to surprise my American friend with a visit, as I used to do all the time back in Ghana. I didn't call because I thought that he would be home at that hour. When I knocked, he opened the front door in surprise. Later when I went to the bathroom, I overheard his mother say, "Doesn't he have your telephone number?" I thought that my visit would be a pleasant surprise, but apparently my actions were unacceptable and I was considered rude.

b. I was walking in my neighborhood with my sister holding hands. We noticed that everybody was staring at us. My sister and I couldn't guess what was the matter. Later my older brother explained that two girls or two boys just don't do that in the United States. I feel sad about this. Sometimes I feel really happy and I want to hold my sister's hand like we used to do back home in Mexico, but I don't dare to. It's not worth being the object of other people's attention.

c. In Korea, when young people ask for permission to go out, the parent wants to know where they are going, who is going to be there, and when they plan to return. Often a phone number must be provided. Young people need their parents' permission and to get this permission, they must give their parents the information asked for. In contrast, here in the United States, teenagers just call their friends and make their own appointments. Teenagers are insulted if a parent asks too many questions.

d. One day I went to my friend's house here in New York. As I entered, my friend's mother went inside her bedroom without saying hello. As I left, I heard her bedroom door open and she came out. This could never happen in Haiti. There if I visit a friend, his mother greets me and engages me in conversation. Without even asking she brings out some food and drinks.

e. Within the traditional Pakistani family, if a parent scolds a child, the child must remain quiet without answering back. This shows the child's respect. In contrast, an American child often responds to his parent when being scolded, perhaps protesting or offering an explanation. This often creates an unfair situation for the Pakistani child. Suppose a child is being scolded unfairly. Perhaps a misunderstanding occurred. The child will feel resentment towards the parent but is unable to clarify the matter.

f. In India we buy fresh foods like fruits and vegetables and dairy products in small quantities every day. Because you go to the market daily, you interact with people a lot. A warm familiarity with your neighbors and the shopkeepers is created. Here in the United States, busy Americans want to save time. They go to supermarkets, huge warehouses of food, and buy enough to last a week or even more. It is convenient but it's all business. You don't get the chance to pass a friendly word with familiar faces.

g. I remember that on my first day of school here, I dressed formally, as I used to do in China. When I got to class, I saw students dressed very casually. Some students were even wearing cut jeans. Some male students had hair as long as a girl's. Everything seemed so strange to me. Later the teacher walked in with a cup of coffee. During his lecture, a student got up and walked out without asking permission or excusing himself. I had never seen this in my country. If a teacher came into class drinking a beverage, the students would be shocked. And even college students must ask permission from the teacher if they want to leave in the middle of a class.

Example *g* in the preceding activity was written by Cui Fang Zhou from China. Unlike Lei, who first planned his essay by making an outline, Cui Fang began her essay on the cultural differences between her homeland and the United States by writing a paragraph describing what she had noticed at school. Later, she added more material, wrote an introduction and a conclusion, and changed the organization, thereby developing the single paragraph into an essay.

DIFFERENT CULTURES

CUI FANG ZHOU

The United States is a land of capitalism where people have great   1
personal freedom. It seems to me that everything here revolves around
money. On the street the topic most frequently overheard is connected
to money. Perhaps related to this is the feeling of freedom that people
have here to do whatever they want to do with little regard to rules of
formality.

As soon as my plane landed at Kennedy Airport in New York I began   2
to understand about the role of money here. I tried to find a cart to carry
my luggage. There were many carts neatly lined up on a rack. I tried to
pull one out but I was unable to. A man came along and said that I had
to deposit money in a box on the rack in order to remove the cart. How
strange, I thought, that the airport did not provide carts free of charge to
the travelers like the international airport back home in Beijing.

I pushed the cart towards the exit gate. A middle-aged man smiled at   3
me and asked me if I needed help. How kind he was, I thought. I certainly did need help maneuvering the cart loaded with two huge suitcases, all my possessions I had brought with me from China for my stay
in the United States while I studied for two years. After he moved the
cart through the gate, he held out his hand to receive his fee. I realized
that he had helped me only because this was his way of earning money.
In China, when a person helps you, he does so not to receive a mone-
tary reward.

These two examples reflect the difference between capitalism and   4
socialism. In Communist China, the government controls the economy.
There is great equality of wealth. There is little opportunity for people to
make money so they don't try. I understand, however, that things are
changing back home as the private economy is developing. It will be interesting to see how changes in economic policy will affect the social
relations.

Another striking difference between the United States and China is   5
the degree of personal freedom here. It seems that in the United States
you can do just about whatever you want to. I remember that on my
first day of college here, I dressed very formally, as I used to do in
China. When I got to class, I saw students dressed very casually. Some
students were even wearing cut jeans. Some male students had hair as
long as a girl's. Everything seemed so strange to me.

The teacher walked in with a cup of coffee. During his lecture, a stu-   6
dent got up and walked out without asking permission or excusing himself. I had never seen this in my country. If a teacher came into class
drinking a beverage, the students would be shocked. And even college
students must ask permission from the teacher if they want to leave in
the middle of a class.

I suppose each way of life has its own pluses and minuses. The im-   7
portant thing is to learn about the culture where you are living and try to
take advantage of the particular opportunities offered.

. . . .

ANALYSIS

1. What is the thesis statement of the essay?

2. How is this essay organized—from general to specific or from specific to general?
   Give specific examples to support your answer.

3. What is the topic sentence of paragraph 2? What material is provided as supporting evidence?

4. Paragraph 4 serves as a transition or connection between the two main themes of
   the essay. In your opinion, does the paragraph help make the essay clearer? Explain.

5. What is the topic sentence of paragraph 5? Give specific examples to support your
   answer.

6. What conclusions has Cui Fang drawn from her experiences?

Now let's look at an analysis of the outline Cui Fang prepared to help her develop
and organize her ideas as she wrote the final version of her essay.

DIFFERENT CULTURES
(Analysis)
CUI FANG ZHOU

Paragraph 1

In her thesis statement Cui Fang introduces the ideas of the importance of money in
the United States and the greater personal freedom here relative to China.

Paragraphs 2 and 3

Paragraph 2 begins with a topic sentence about the role of money. The supporting evidence for this generalization includes the incidents involving the luggage cart in the airport.

Paragraph 4

This serves as a transition between the two themes of the essay: the role of money and the degree of personal freedom.

Paragraphs 5 and 6

Paragraph 5 starts with a topic sentence about the degree of personal freedom. A number of observations made at school support Cui Fang's generalization.

Paragraph 7

In her conclusion, Cui Fang recognizes that each way of life has its advantages and disadvantages.

Essay Writing

. . . .

GENERATING IDEAS

Freewrite about the cultural differences you have observed between the United States and your homeland. You may want to use the categories below, but feel free to consider anything related to the topic.

a. the nature of social relationships

b. personal freedom

c. acceptable public behavior

d. the effects of the economic system

e. the role of family

f. raising and educating children

g. respect for privacy

h. the pace of life

. . . .

ASSIGNMENT

Use your freewriting as the basis of an essay about an important cultural difference between the United States and your homeland. Like Lei, you may want to make an outline of your ideas before you write your first draft. Or you may prefer to approach the assignment as Cui Fang did: write your first draft and then prepare an outline to help you develop and organize your ideas as you revise. If you have difficulty developing and organizing your ideas, review the outlines Lei and Cui Fang used to help them write their successful essays. After you have written an early draft, share it with a teacher or a friend and explore possible revisions that would make it even more successful.

6

CHANGES

· · · · · · · · · · · · · · · · ·

The Talmud—the great collection of Jewish law—tells of an illiterate shepherd who stopped by a stream with his thirsty flock. There he noticed that the steady flow of water had carved a deep groove into the rock where the water was emerging from an underground spring. "If the flowing water can carve out an impression in solid rock," he thought, "perhaps there is yet hope that with time and patience I might become a learned man." So inspired, the shepherd went to Jerusalem, where he studied for many years and eventually became the leading scholar of his day.

Sometimes change is gradual; sometimes sudden. How has your life changed since coming to the United States?

In this chapter you will read the *lyrics,* or words, to two popular songs. The first deals specifically with the immigrant experience; the second looks at the theme of change in a more universal context.

READING

The Greenhorn Cousin

· · · · · · · · · · · · · · · · ·

ESTABLISHING THE CONTEXT

Jews have been a part of the American landscape since the beginnings of the European settlement in the New World. The largest influx of Jewish immigrants—more than 2 million—came from Eastern Europe in the period from 1880 to the start of World War I, joining their coreligionists who had come from Holland and Germany in previous generations.

The restrictive immigration policy following World War I reduced immigration to the United States to a trickle. During World War II, Nazi Germany initiated the "final solution" to Europe's "Jewish problem." With no place to flee, more than 6 million men, women, and children perished in the *Holocaust,* the extermination of Jews by the Nazis and their collaborators. In the postwar years, as restrictions were relaxed, thousands of survivors joined the other displaced persons of Europe coming to the United States. More recently, with the thawing of the cold war and the breakup of the former Soviet Union, Jews have once again come in significant numbers to the United States.

"The Greenhorn Cousin" was a popular song from the Jewish theater, which flourished in New York City in the first decades of this century. The song was originally written in Yiddish, the language spoken by more than 8 million of the world's 10 million Jews at the time. Today the vitality of the language has all but disappeared.

· · · · · · · · · · · · · · · ·

TO BEGIN

1. A *greenhorn* is a newly arrived immigrant. What might be the *etymology,* or origin, of the word? Try to make an educated guess; then consult an un-abridged dictionary and read the etymological notes under the entry for the word.

2. Before you begin reading, look up the definitions of two words that appear in the song if you are not familiar with them: *millinery* and *grimace.*

3. Read the last line of the song. Using your own experiences as well as what you have learned in school and from other sources, create a possible *scenario,* a brief description of a story, that would lead an immigrant to have such a negative feel-ing about the United States.

You will probably find that the vocabulary used in "The Greenhorn Cousin"—apart from the few words noted above—is less challenging than it is in the other sec-tions you have read to this point. Why might you expect the language of popular song to be particularly accessible?

THE GREENHORN COUSIN

Once a cousin came to me,
Pretty as gold was she, the greenhorn,
Her cheeks like red oranges,
Her tiny feet begging to dance.

She didn't walk, she skipped along,
She didn't talk, she sang,
Her manner was gay and cheerful,
That's how my cousin used to be.

I found a place with my neighbor,
The one who has a millinery store,
I got a job for my cousin,
Blessed be the golden land.

Since then many years have passed.
My cousin has become a wreck
From many years of collecting wages
Till nothing was left of her.

Underneath her pretty blue eyes
Black lines are drawn,

Her cheeks, once like red oranges,
Have now turned entirely green.

Today, when I meet my cousin
And ask her: "How are you, greenhorn?"
She answers with a grimace,
"To the devil with Columbus's land!"

. . . .

RESPONSE AND ANALYSIS

1. Write for a few minutes in response to what you have read. Besides summarizing, you may want to explore your feelings and thoughts about the reading. It may be helpful to consider these categories:

   a. what you understood about the reading

   b. something that puzzled you in the reading

   c. something you would like to discuss with the writer or one of the characters

   d. a memory the reading evoked

   e. how you felt about the reading

2. Because a song is often relatively short, much information must be packed into a few words. "The Greenhorn Cousin" has only twenty-four lines, organized into six *verses,* yet it manages to convey a complete narrative. Where in the song can the following information be found?

   a. a physical description of the cousin when she first came here

   b. a description of the cousin's personality when she first came here

   c. an early opinion about life in the United States

   d. the passing of time from the past to the present

   e. changes that have occurred in the cousin

   f. her present opinion of the United States

3. Identify and explain the two similes in the song.

4. In many parts of the world, there is a tradition of using song to protest social or economic conditions or to express a position on a political issue. "The Greenhorn Cousin" was written at a time when labor unions were gaining strength in the United States as American workers sought to improve their wages and working conditions. Bring in the words (in translation!) to a protest or topical song from your homeland, if such a tradition exists.

READING

Changes

PHIL OCHS

. . . .

ESTABLISHING THE CONTEXT

The American tradition of musical protest reached a peak in the 1960s, when many songs were written to protest United States involvement in Viet Nam and discriminatory policies against African Americans and other oppressed peoples. One of the most political of the singer-songwriters was Phil Ochs, an activist who wrote dozens of protest songs. Not all of his songs, however, were topical; others, like "Changes," were in the tradition of *lyrical poetry*, expressing deeply felt emotions.

. . . .

TO BEGIN

You have used freewriting in your journals as a way to generate ideas for your essays and to respond to what you have read. Freewriting is also appropriate before you begin reading. As you freewrite you gather your prior knowledge and ideas on a given topic. The more you bring to the reading, the more accessible it becomes. Reflect on the title of the song, "Changes." Then freewrite on the topic of change for a number of minutes. After you have completed the reading, you can check to see if you were able to anticipate the themes explored in the song.

Like "The Greenhorn Cousin," "Changes" is relatively short and will probably contain less challenging vocabulary than the preceding selections. The language is characterized by a number of techniques commonly found in poems and songs. As you read the words to the song, do you notice any phrases you find especially appealing?

CHANGES

PHIL OCHS

Sit by my side, come as close as the air,
Share in a mem'ry of grey,
And wander in my words. And dream about
The pictures that I play of changes.

Green leaves of summer turn red in the fall,
To brown and to yellow they fade,
And then they have to die, trapped within
The circle time parade of changes.

Scenes of my young years were warm in my mind,
Visions of shadows that shine.
Till one day I returned and found they were
The victims of the vines of changes.

The world's spinning madly, it drifts in the dark,
Swings through a hollow of haze.
A race around the stars, a journey through
The universe ablaze with changes.

Moments of magic will glow in the night.
All fears of the forest are gone.
But when the morning breaks, they're swept away
By golden drops of dawn of changes.

Passions will part to strange melody
As fires will sometimes burn cold.
Like petals in the wind, we're puppets
To the silver strings of souls of changes.

Your tears will be trembling, now we're somewhere else.
One last cup of wine we will pour.
And I'll kiss you one more time and leave you
On the rolling river shores of changes.

So sit by my side, come as close as the air,
Share in a mem'ry of grey,
And wander in my words. And dream about
The pictures that I play of changes.

. . . .

RESPONSE AND ANALYSIS

1. Write for a few minutes in response to what you have read. Besides summarizing, you may want to explore your feelings and thoughts about the reading. It may be helpful to consider these categories:

    a. what you understood about the reading

b. something that puzzled you in the reading

c. something you would like to discuss with the writer or one of the characters

d. a memory the reading evoked

e. how you felt about the reading

2. Who sings the song? To whom?

3. The verses of the song explore the theme of change as reflected in the human experience and in the world of nature. For example, verse 2 recalls the change of seasons. What other kinds of changes are explored in the song? Were you able to anticipate any in your freewriting?

4. Identify and explain the two similes in the song.

5. Notice that the first verse is repeated as the conclusion to the song. Why do you think this is done?

. . . .

FURTHER EXPLORATION OF LANGUAGE AND LITERATURE: ALLITERATION AND METAPHOR

Alliteration

Poets and songwriters use a variety of techniques to make the sound of their words more pleasing. You are probably familiar with the element of rhyme in poetry and song. Another important element is *alliteration,* the appearance of the same sound at the beginning of two or more words next to or close to each other. "Changes" opens with an alliterative phrase: "Sit by my side"; the *s* sound is repeated. Later in the first verse, the phrase "wander in my words" is also alliterative.

1. Make a list of the other examples of alliteration found in the song.

2. Is alliteration used in the popular songs or poems in your native language? Are you able to come up with a few examples of alliteration from your native language or from popular American songs with which you are familiar?

Metaphor

Both songs in this chapter contain similes. Because the word *like* or *as* is used in this figure of speech, the comparison is *explicit,* or stated directly. If you read carefully, it is usually not too difficult to identify and explain similes such as "cheeks as red as oranges" (in "The Greenhorn Cousin") or "passions will part . . . as fires will sometimes turn cold" (in "Changes").

A far more subtle figure of speech is the metaphor, a comparison without the words *like* or *as.* Because these words are not used, the comparison is *implicit,* or suggested, and you may not even notice that one is used. For example, in verse 3 of "Changes," the writer recalls scenes from his childhood and laments that they had become "victims of the vines of changes." As a vine grows it may wrap around another plant or tree, taking its food and water, thereby killing it. Similarly, the passing of time can make you a stranger to the memory of people and places that were dear to you years earlier.

Explain the other metaphors used in "Changes":

a. trapped within the circle time parade of changes

b. we're puppets to the silver strings of souls of changes

c. the rolling river shores of changes

Student Essay

In the previous chapter you read an essay by Cui Fang Zhou in which she discusses some of the cultural differences between the United States and China. In the following essay Cui Fang explores the theme of change when she considers what she has gained and what she has lost by coming to live in the United States.

THE RIGHT DECISION?

CUI FANG ZHOU

Coming to America is the dream of people throughout the world. However, it doesn't mean that everything is gained by coming here; you gain in some ways but lose in others. I think that life is not perfect no matter where you live.   1

My life has changed a great deal since I have come to America. I am no longer an office worker; instead I am now working as a cashier in a restaurant. When I was living in China, I used to work for a research institute as a mechanical designer. I got good benefits from the institute. But when I first came here, I could not get a good job because my English was poor. I could only find employment in low-skill fields like restaurant work. These were very hard jobs with low pay, far from the ones I once did in China.   2

I have also given up much in my social and family life. During the holidays I become homesick. I feel that I have lost my family, lost the happiness of family gatherings. I remember each big holiday in China.   3

My grandmother was always the first guest to arrive at the house. She would always come with gifts: shoes or clothing for the children, herbal medicines for my mother and father, and wine for the dinner. She would chat with us about distant relatives we had not heard from in some time. My mother was usually busy preparing as many as ten dishes in the kitchen for the holiday dinner: chicken, duck, fish, and pork, with rice and Chinese vegetables I haven't seen here in the United States. After dinner, the women would drink wine, the men would drink beer or strong liquor, and everyone would have sweet cakes. Sometimes my friends came over and we went to a movie together.

When I think of these things, I feel that I have lost a lot by coming to   4
America. Sometimes I want to go back to China. However, when I consider other things, I begin to feel that coming to America has been worth it.

Coming to America has given me the chance to get a good education.   5
In China you have to score very high on the college entrance examinations if you want to study in the university. Otherwise you can only study at a less prestigious vocational or technical school. If I had stayed in China I wouldn't have been able to go to college. Moreover, living, working, and studying here has given me the opportunity to learn about other people and this has helped me to understand my own culture.

I also feel that life in America is freer than in China. In China, when I   6
wanted to do something, I not only considered my own feelings, but I also had to consider other people's opinions. For example, here in the United States a woman can wear a low-cut blouse or tight pants. People will not express disapproval of the way she dresses. Couples can embrace and kiss in public. If I hadn't come to the United States, I believe that I wouldn't have felt as comfortable as I now do. Nobody criticizes me whatever I wear or however I behave. I don't have to spend a lot of time thinking about what other people think of me.

Obviously, coming to America has let me gain a lot, despite the   7
losses. Hopefully, I can gain more in the future if I continue to stay in America. I hope to eliminate all doubts as to whether coming to America has really been worth it.

. . . .

RESPONSE AND ANALYSIS

1. How has Cui Fang organized her essay? Make your analysis paragraph by paragraph using these terms: *introduction, thesis statement, topic sentence* and *supporting material, transition,* and *conclusion.*

2. There is no explicit mention of Cui Fang's age nor how long she has been in the United States. However, this information is implicit in the contents of the essay. How old would you suppose Cui Fang is? How long has she been in the United States? Bring specific evidence from the essay to support your answer. In your opinion, would the essay have been more successful had this background information been given explicitly and not implicitly? Explain.

Focus on Writing: Changing the Organization

You have seen that revision usually involves changing the contents of your essay, either by adding or by omitting material. Sometimes, however, you may be able to present the same material more clearly by organizing it into paragraphs differently.

Let's look at an early draft of Cui Fang Zhou's essay. Notice that although the contents of the two versions are essentially the same, she has changed the way the essay is organized into paragraphs.

CHANGES
(Early Draft)
CUI FANG ZHOU

Coming to America is the dream of people throughout the world.   1
However, it doesn't mean that everything is gained by coming here; you gain in some ways but lose in others. I think that life is not perfect no matter where you live.

My life has changed a great deal since I have come to America. I am   2
no longer an office worker; instead I am now working as a cashier. When I was living in China, I used to work for a research institute as a mechanical designer. I got good benefits from the institute. But when I first came here I could not get a good job because my English was poor. I could only find work in low skill fields like restaurant work. These were very hard jobs with low pay, far from the ones I once did in China.

During a holiday, I become homesick. I feel that I have lost my fam-   3
ily and lost the happiness of family gatherings. I remember each big holiday in China. My grandmother was always the first guest to arrive at my house. She would always come with gifts: shoes or clothing for the children, herbal medicines for my mother and father, and wine for the dinner. She would chat with us about distant relatives we had not heard

from in some time. My mother was usually busy preparing as many as ten dishes in the kitchen for the holiday dinner: chicken, duck, fish, and pork with rice and Chinese vegetables I haven't seen here in the United States. After dinner, the women would drink wine, the men would drink beer or strong liquor, and everyone would have sweet cakes. Sometimes my friends came over and we went to a movie together. When I think of these things, I feel that I have lost a lot by coming to America. Sometimes I want to go back to China. However, when I consider other things, I begin to feel that coming to America has been worth it. Coming to America has given me the chance to get a good education. In China you have to score very high on the college entrance examinations if you want to study in the university. Otherwise you can only study at a less prestigious vocational or technical school. If I had stayed in China, I wouldn't have been able to go to college. Moreover, living, working, and studying here has given me the opportunity to learn about other people and this has helped me to understand my own culture.

I also feel that life in America is freer than in China. In China, when I   4
wanted to do something, I not only considered my own feelings, but I also had to consider other people's opinions. For example, here in the United States, a woman can wear a low cut blouse or tight pants. People will not express disapproval of the way she dresses. Couples can embrace and kiss in public. If I hadn't come to the United States, I believe that I wouldn't have felt as comfortable as I now do. Nobody criticizes me whatever I wear or however I behave. I don't have to spend a lot of time thinking about what other people think of me.

Obviously, coming to America has let me gain a lot, despite the   5
losses. Hopefully, I can gain more in the future if I continue to stay in America. I hope that I will be able to eliminate all doubts as to whether coming to America has really been worth it.

. . . .

ANALYSIS

1. How had Cui Fang organized the early draft of her essay? Make your analysis paragraph by paragraph using the same terms you used earlier in your analysis of the final version: *introduction, thesis statement, topic sentence* and *supporting material, transition,* and *conclusion.*

2. Compare the two analyses. How has Cui Fang reorganized the same material in the final version of her essay?

3. Notice that Cui Fang has also given a different title to the final version of her essay. Why do you think she made the change? Which title do you prefer? Explain.

4. For further practice, go back to the essays you have written. Revise any essay that you feel could be made more effective by organizing your material into paragraphs differently.

Essay Writing

. . . .

GENERATING IDEAS

Another way to generate ideas for an essay is to *brainstorm*. When you brainstorm you list all the possible ideas you and the people you are working with can think of that are relevant to the topic you are considering. After your list is compiled, you choose those ideas that are most appealing.

Although this is not a grammar book, to help you brainstorm ideas for an essay about how you and your life have changed since coming to the United States, it may be helpful to consider two concepts from English grammar: *habitual aspect* and the *contrary-to-fact condition*.

Habitual Aspect

When Cui Fang writes in paragraph 2, "I used to work for a research institute . . . ," she means that she worked there regularly for an indeterminate number of weeks, months, or even years. In grammatical terminology, this idea is referred to as *habitual aspect*. To convey habitual aspect in the past tense, Cui Fang uses the construction "used to."

Another way to convey habitual aspect is with the construction "would." Cui Fang writes in paragraph 3 that her grandmother "would always come with gifts." She means that it was her grandmother's habit to come with gifts; not only did she come with gifts on that one occasion, but she came with gifts many times. Cui Fang conveys habitual aspect again later in the paragraph when she writes, "After dinner, the women would drink wine, the men would drink beer or strong liquor, and everyone would have sweet cakes."

For an essay about how you and your life have changed since coming to the United States, it is logical to compare and contrast the different periods in your life. You might include some description of how your life used to be and explore some of the things you would (or would not) do back home. To do this, use the two constructions—*used to* and *would*—that convey habitual aspect.

The Contrary-to-Fact Condition

When Cui Fang writes in paragraph 5, "If I had stayed in China I wouldn't have been able to go to college," she is referring to an idea that is contrary to what actually happened. Because she didn't stay in China and she did come here, she has been able to go to college. The grammatical construction she uses to express this idea is called the *contrary-to-fact condition*. She later uses the same construction in paragraph 6 when she writes, "If I hadn't come to the United States, I believe that I wouldn't have felt as comfortable as I now do."

Again, for an essay about how you and your life have changed since coming to the United States, it is logical to talk about how things would have been had you remained home. To do this, use the contrary-to-fact condition.

The sentence patterns that follow employ habitual aspect and the contrary-to-fact condition. Use them to help you generate ideas for an essay about how you and your life have changed since coming to the United States. Try to come up with as many examples as you can.

1. In my country I would (not) _____.
   Here in the United States _____.

Example

In Peru I would play soccer every Saturday. Here in the United States I am unable to because I am so busy working and studying.

2. Back home in_____, I (never) used to
   _____. Since coming to the United States,
   I_____.

Example

Back home in Taiwan I never used to be afraid to go out late at night. Since coming to the United States, I have become very cautious about traveling alone in certain parts of my city, even during the day.

3. If I had stayed in _____, I probably
   would (not) have _____.

Example

If I had stayed in Russia, I probably would not have been able to study at the university.

4. If I hadn't immigrated to the United States, I probably
   would (not) have_____.

Example

If I hadn't immigrated to the United States, I probably would have been drafted into the Nicaraguan Army and fought in the civil war against the Sandinistas.

. . . .

ASSIGNMENT

Use the ideas you generated in the previous brainstorming activity as the basis of an essay about how you and your life have changed as a result of coming to the United States. As with freewriting, you will not be able to include all your ideas. You must decide what to develop and what to omit. As you try to organize your material, keep in mind the way Cui Fang organized her material into paragraphs in the final version of her essay: she includes an explicit thesis statement in the introduction, then explores each main idea in a different paragraph, which includes a topic sentence and supporting material. After you have written an early draft of your essay, share it with a teacher or a friend and explore possible revisions that would make it even more successful.

PHOTOGRAPHS

. . . .

Many students enjoy sharing their carefully arranged photograph albums with their classmates. Which of your personal photographs are especially significant to you?

READING FROM

The Lonely Crossing of Juan Cabrera

J. JOAQUÍN FRAXEDAS

. . . .

ESTABLISHING THE CONTEXT

In the summer of 1994, thousands of Cubans fled their homeland on homemade rafts in an attempt to cross a ninety-mile stretch of ocean and reach the large expatriate Cuban community in Florida. For several weeks, the United States Coast Guard was on order to intercept the *balseros,* or rafters, and detain them at the American naval base at Guantanamo Bay, Cuba. The mass exodus was abruptly brought to a stop when the governments of the two countries signed an agreement that allowed for the annual legal immigration of twenty thousand Cubans to the United States.

You may recall the historical reference to Cuba and the Cuban Missile Crisis in *How the García Girls Lost Their Accents* (chapter 3). If you investigated that reference further, you no doubt read about the revolution led by Fidel Castro, who took control of the Cuban government in 1959. As Castro's vision of Cuba and his Communist sympathies became clear, more than a quarter-million Cubans would flee to the United States. Many settled in Dade County, Florida, which would soon become the center of Cuban culture in the United States. Then for nearly three decades, apart from a few weeks in 1980 when restrictions were temporarily relaxed, most Cubans who managed to leave had to do so illegally. The agreement of 1994 guarantees an increased Cuban immigrant presence in the United States.

J. Joaquín Fraxedas is a Cuban American who came to the United States at the age of ten, shortly after the revolution in his homeland. A lawyer by profession, Fraxedas is also a trained pilot who has participated in many rescues of Cuban *balseros* lost at sea. In *The Lonely Crossing of Juan Cabrera,* his first novel, Fraxedas tells the story of three Cuban men who try to flee the country they now find intolerable. In the excerpt below, Juan and his friends Andrés and Raúl are making the final preparations for their escape.

. . . .

TO BEGIN

1. You will probably come across some unfamiliar words in this excerpt from *The Lonely Crossing of Juan Cabrera*. Sometimes it helps to familiarize yourself with key vocabulary before you begin reading. The underlined words in the following passages are all related to the ocean the men must cross and the raft they are using to make their escape. Try to determine the meaning of each word or phrase by its context. Then provide a dictionary definition either in English or in your native language.

    a. An hour later Raúl brought the <u>inner tubes</u> and the <u>air pump</u> from the car and spread them out on the floor of the bungalow. Juan and Andrés took turns pumping air into the tubes. . . .

    b. They <u>lashed</u> the inner tubes in a straight line and strapped the <u>tarpaulin</u> over them. They had dragged the <u>raft</u> into the <u>surf</u> and were about to push off when Raúl decided to go back to the car.

    c. Raúl finished tying the lines, threw the <u>paddles</u> on the raft, and the three of them <u>waded</u> deeper into the water, holding on to the lashings. Soon they were drifting eastward along the coast with the outgoing <u>tide</u>.

    d. When Juan and Raúl finished eating, Andrés untied a bottle of water he had fastened to an <u>eyelet on the canvas</u> with some cord, and handed it to Raúl.

2. Based on the sentences from the previous activity, try to make a sketch of the raft that Juan and his friends have constructed.

3. If you were making such an escape, what sorts of things would you take along? Explain.

There will probably be other unfamiliar words in this excerpt from *The Lonely Crossing of Juan Cabrera*. Remember, however, that you can still enjoy and understand what you read without knowing the definition of every word. Try to use the context to guess at the unfamiliar words and phrases as you read for your interest and pleasure about the attempted escape of Juan and his friends. Don't be overly concerned with words and phrases you don't understand; there will be another vocabulary activity to do after you read, respond to, and analyze the selection.

FROM

THE LONELY CROSSING OF JUAN CABRERA

J. JOAQUÍN FRAXEDAS

The sun was setting behind them now as they drove toward Guanabo,   1 following the shoreline. To the east the ocean showed deep purple with shades of violet far off in the distance.

It was dark by the time they arrived at Andrés's place and drove   2
down the narrow, winding dirt road that led to his little bungalow near
the water. The road was lined with tall weeds, and Juan could see the
reflection from the headlights shining on the upraised eyes of the big
land crabs that came out of their burrows at night and now scurried out
of the way as the car approached.

"*¡Aquí!* Over here!" called Andrés as Juan went to knock on the door   3
of the bungalow. Andrés was returning from the water's edge, limping
barefoot on the coarse sand.

"Just checking the water," he whispered with an impish smile as he   4
came up to them.

"Well, how is it?" asked Raúl.   5

"Nice and warm—like bathwater."   6

"Let's not speak out here," said Juan.   7

"Yes, yes, of course, *entren,* come in, please," Andrés said, opening   8
the door.

Inside Andrés's bungalow, a bare light bulb dangled on a black wire   9
several feet from the ceiling at the center of the room. When the men
came in, the breeze from the ocean set the bulb in motion, casting their
swaying shadows on the blue walls. Three backpacks were stacked
neatly in a corner next to three glass bottles filled with water. Above the
bottles, three rough-hewn wooden paddles were leaning against the
wall.

"Everything is ready," Andrés said as soon as they walked in.   10

"Have you seen any guards?" asked Juan.   11

"Yes, I just saw two with German shepherds down by the   12
water."

In the harsh light from the bare bulb, Andrés looked old and frail,   13
and Juan wondered if he was strong enough now to make the crossing.
Twelve years as a political prisoner at Combinado del Este had aged
him beyond his fifty-five years. His face was as wrinkled as that of a
man in his eighties. Two of his teeth were missing, had got in the way of
a rifle butt. And the leg they broke during the interrogation had never
set right. But his spirit was fine. They never touched that. They never
even came close.

And tonight Andrés was as sprightly as Juan had ever seen him. Talk-   14
ing about the escape, his eyes lit up like a child's on Christmas Eve. He
kept saying, "I can't wait to see Margarita. I just can't wait to see Margarita."

No use trying to persuade him to stay, Juan thought.   15

"Have you boys eaten? Don't have much, but no reason to leave   16
anything behind. I could heat black beans and a little rice," said Andrés.

"I'll have some," said Raúl.   17

"You better eat too, Juan. You'll need your strength," said Andrés.   18

"Do you have any rum?" Raúl asked.   19

"I have a bottle in the cabinet. Would you like me to pour you   20
some?"

"No, but let me have the bottle. I'm going out to check on the guard   21
situation while you heat the food."

Half an hour later Raúl returned, smelling of rum.   22

"Wouldn't take the bottle," he said.   23

"You didn't make them suspicious?" asked Juan.   24

"No. Spilled some rum on my shirt and sat there on the sand acting   25
miserable until they found me. Told them my wife ran off with another
man while I was in Angola."

"Can't believe your *cojones*," said Juan. "You sure they didn't get   26
suspicious?"

"Yes, I'm sure. We spoke of Africa. Showed them my medals. Told   27
them how many imperialists I had killed and what a shock it was to get
back home and find my wife gone. I think they truly felt sorry for me."

"Come on and eat before it gets cold," said Andrés.   28

They sat on *taburetes*—rustic wooden chairs—at a small table   29
pushed against the wall next to the paddles, and ate the beans and rice.
Raúl passed the rum around the table and each of them took a few
swigs out of the bottle.

"Better wait till they move down the beach before we get the things   30
from the car," said Juan.

"Did you get everything?" Andrés asked.   31

"Yes," Juan said. "But we had a close call."   32

"Trouble?"   33

"Not really," said Raúl. "Stopped around Tarara by the G-2. Young   34
kid. Didn't look old enough to carry a gun. He was more scared than
we were. Isn't that right, Juan?"

"Yes," Juan said. "He sure looked scared. Didn't see anything, either.   35
We hid the stuff under the backseat." For a moment Juan felt ashamed
to lie like that and pretend he had not been afraid. But he was used to
lying by now, and soon he got over the unpleasantness and the shame.

An hour later Raúl brought the inner tubes and the air pump from the   36 car and spread them out on the floor of the bungalow. Juan and Andrés took turns pumping air into the tubes while Raúl made trips to the car, picking up odds and ends.

"Better lash them together after we get to the beach," said Raúl. "Too   37
awkward to take it out the door after it's put together."

"They might see us working out there," said Juan.   38

"Just have to take that chance," Raúl said. "In fact, don't pump them   39
up too big here. We'll finish pumping them up at the beach. They won't
get through the door if you pump them too big."

After sunset, clouds had moved in from the northwest and it was   40
overcast and pitch black out by the water. They laid the inner tubes in a
row on the coarse sand and finished pumping air into them. Every few
seconds Juan stopped and looked over his shoulder. The squeaking
noise the pump made each time he pushed in the rusty cylinder
sounded much louder out here, and any moment he expected to see
one of the guards looming over him, a growling German shepherd at his
side.

They lashed the inner tubes in a straight line and strapped the tarpau-   41
lin over them. They had dragged the raft into the surf and were about to
push off when Raúl decided to go back to the car.

"What the hell are you doing now?" Juan whispered.   42

"Just going to get a couple more lines. Be right back."   43

As Raúl came back with the lines, Juan saw a flashlight coming   44
around a point off in the distance.

"Hurry, hurry, they're coming back," he whispered, on the verge of   45
panic.

Raúl finished tying the lines, threw the paddles on the raft, and the   46
three of them waded deeper into the water, holding on to the lashings.
Soon they were drifting eastward along the coast with the outgoing tide.

By midnight the sound of barking dogs on the beach, and of an occa-   47
sional passing truck, and all the other sounds of the shore that had been
with them for the first few hours after they put in, had faded and died,
like the glow of Havana on the horizon that had vanished behind them
in the enveloping gloom.

None of them had ever been at sea. And now their eyes were fixed   48
on the dark water, the rhythmic splashing of the paddles mesmerizing
them, as they sat on the awkward raft. No one spoke. There were only
the sounds of the sea.

By the time the overcast began to clear from the northwest, the pad-   49 dles had grown heavy and blisters had formed on their hands. As the sea slowly turned gray with the first hint of dawn, Raúl and Andrés began to nod off.

Only Juan was still paddling when the stars above the eastern horizon dimmed with the coming sun. His eyes turned north to the rising stars of the Great Bear and then overhead to the tight Pleiades cluster, which was fading rapidly in the soft light. The wind was fair and warm and blew from the south.   50

A proper boat would have been easier to navigate, he thought. But a boat would have increased their chances of being detected and captured. Besides, where could they have gotten a boat? And if they had managed to find a boat, where would they have hidden it while they made their preparations and collected each item needed for the crossing? The truth is, the raft served them well. It was as fine an inner-tube raft as ever attempted the crossing.   51

Juan thought about the native Cubans who had lived in the island before Columbus arrived. He remembered studying about them while he was still in elementary school, before the revolution, before everything changed. He thought about how the Tainos and the other, more primitive tribe, the Siboneys, plied these same waters in canoes dug from the trunks of their sacred ceiba trees hundreds of years before the Spanish came and discovered the green islands of the Caribbean. He remembered looking at the sea through the window in his classroom and imagining what it must have been like to kneel in a shallow dugout canoe, paddling out toward the horizon as the color of the water changed from a crystal aquamarine near the shore to a profound dark blue over the fantastic trenches and basins of the ocean floor, where steep walls drop thousands and thousands of feet to a place that is dark and cold, where the water never mixes with other, warmer waters.   52

Juan thought about these things and he thought about the girl with the dark hair and radiant blue eyes who was now in Miami. Then he eased his lean, muscular body into a reclining position on the canvas and fell asleep listening to the muffled sound of the water lapping against the inner tubes. He dreamed of sweet-smelling green fields of sugarcane, and his dream was so vivid that he heard the rustling of the cane in the wind and then, later in his dream, he heard the sound of hard, driving rain beating down on the tall stalks of cane.   53

As the morning brought the colors back to the sea, birds came from   54 their nesting places in the river estuaries along the north coast, looking for fish. A pair of terns circled with intense concentration, one or the other occasionally diving into the warm, silky water near the raft.

Later the breeze picked up, giving the water a light chop, and dol- 55 phins began to feed on a school of mackerel north of the raft. The dolphins worked in concert, herding the mackerel into a tight circle. The mackerel churned the water inside the circle, and their frenzied movements made a sound like the rain makes when it falls on the sea. The sky was brilliant blue and broken only by a few feathery cirrus clouds moving fast to the northwest.

Two burly arms shook Juan awake. "How far have we come?" asked 56 a groggy voice behind him.

"We came far in the night," Juan answered as he yawned. "At least 57 twelve miles, maybe more. The outgoing tide helped."

Raúl was sitting on the inner tube lashed behind Juan's. He was lean- 58 ing back now, looking at the feathery clouds. As he sat there, with his massive legs and arms and shoulders spilling over the sides of the inner tube, he looked absurd, almost comical, Juan thought.

"*Bueno,* well, I guess even if we wanted to, we couldn't go back 59 now," said Raúl.

"Damn right," said Juan. "We beat the *contra-corriente.* We are in 60 the main stream. We can't turn back."

The *contra-corriente* is what Cubans call the currents that spin off the 61 Gulf Stream, like eddies, and sometimes push you back toward the coast.

Andrés was now beginning to stir. 62

"Who's going back?" he asked, his eyes still closed. "Are we going 63 back?"

"Nobody's going back, Andrés," said Juan. "We're just talking about 64 the *contra-corriente.* We beat it last night and now we are in the great stream; we can't turn back."

"Good," said Andrés, rubbing his eyes. "I was afraid we were going 65 back. Is anybody hungry?"

"Sure," said Raúl. "I'm starving. What have you got there?" 66

Andrés took out a can of Russian meat and a rusty can opener from 67 his knapsack, which was strapped to the raft with the same line they used to secure the tarpaulin to the inner tubes. He opened the can and handed it to Raúl, saying, "Here, eat some of this. Give some to Juan, too."

"Aren't you going to have any?" Raúl asked. 68

"No. I'm not hungry. You and Juan eat well and finish it up." 69

When Juan and Raúl finished eating, Andrés untied a bottle of water 70 that he had fastened to an eyelet on the canvas with some cord, and handed it to Raúl.

"Drink up, boys, you're going to need your strength to paddle this 71 old man all the way to Miami!" he said, and his eyes brightened.

Andrés then reached into his knapsack and pulled out a creased 72 clear plastic bag. The bag was folded over several times and held together with rubber bands. He removed the rubber bands and slowly unfolded the plastic. From the bag he took out a small Bible with a worn red leather cover and opened it to the place where he kept a photograph. The photograph was black and white and faded and showed a little girl about seven years old, with a big smile and cheerful dark eyes. Andrés turned the photograph over and read the name and the date scrawled in pencil on the back in a child's handwriting: *Margarita, October 29, 1967.* He then ran his fingers over the name and remembered the day his daughter wrote it—a bright Sunday, twenty-three years ago, the day before she left for Miami. His shirt, unbuttoned to the waist, was fluttering in the light breeze. The breeze felt pleasant on his skin, and in the warmth of the morning sun, Andrés was happier than he had been in many years.

. . . .

RESPONSE AND ANALYSIS

1. Write for a few minutes in response to what you have read. Besides summarizing, you may want to explore your feelings and thoughts about the reading. It may be helpful to consider these categories:

   a. what you understood about the reading

   b. something that puzzled you in the reading

   c. something you would like to discuss with the writer or one of the characters

   d. a memory the reading evoked

   e. how you felt about the reading

2. Throughout the story, there are references to the sights and sounds of the ocean. List as many of these as you can find.

3. As you would expect, Juan, Andrés, and Raúl are fearful of being seen by the bor-

der guards as they prepare to make their escape. What steps do the three men take in order to make their escape as inconspicuous as possible?

4. What does Andrés hope to accomplish by mentioning his military service in Africa? Using an encyclopedia or other source, prepare a short report on Cuban military involvement on that continent.

5. Make a list of the thoughts Juan has as he keeps watch while his companions sleep.

6. Although a boat would have been easier to navigate, Juan believes that the raft has advantages. List the advantages that Juan associates with the raft.

7. Discuss the photograph mentioned at the end of the selection. Who is Margarita? How long has she been separated from her father? How might so long a separation between father and daughter be explained?

. . . .

FURTHER EXPLORATION OF LANGUAGE AND LITERATURE: ITALICS

You may have noticed that a number of words in the excerpt from *The Lonely Crossing of Juan Cabrera* appear in a distinct style of printing called *italics*. In paragraph 3, for example, the word *aquí* has been *italicized*, or printed in italics. If you noticed the italicized words, then they have served their purpose: to draw your attention. In this case, italics have been used to emphasize the Spanish words that appear in a text that is otherwise in English. Notice, too, that because the book has been written for the general reader who might not know Spanish, the English equivalent of *aquí*— "over here"—has been supplied.

1. Skim the selection again and locate all the italicized words that are not part of the regular English *lexicon*, or vocabulary. Has the English equivalent been supplied for each?

2. Italics have a variety of uses, apart from indicating foreign words and phrases. Skim this textbook and locate other examples of italicization. For each example, explain why the italics have been selected.

A final note about italics: unless you use a word processor that allows you to manipulate different *fonts*, or styles of print, you will have to use underlining in place of italics. Many of the model essays you have read were written by students who did not have access to such a word processor. These student writers simply underlined the titles and words that otherwise would have been written in italics.

· · · · · · · · · · · · · · · ·

VOCABULARY: ADJECTIVES

From your study of English grammar you are probably familiar with the term *adjective,* a descriptive word. Adjectives are used with particular effectiveness in the excerpt. In the following passages, try to determine the meaning of each underlined adjective by its context. (You may want to choose additional words from the selection if you found the vocabulary very challenging.) Then provide a dictionary definition either in English or in your native language. Finally, read the excerpt from *The Lonely Crossing of Juan Cabrera* a second time, paying close attention to the words you have learned as well as the other points discussed in the previous activities.

1. "Just checking the water," he whispered with an impish smile as he came up to them.

2. In the harsh light from the bare bulb, Andrés looked old and frail, and Juan wondered if he was strong enough now to make the crossing.

3. And tonight Andrés was as sprightly as Juan had ever seen him.

4. "Better lash them together after we get to the beach," said Raúl. "Too awkward to take it out the door after it's put together."

5. They laid the inner tubes in a row on the coarse sand and finished pumping air into them.

6. And now their eyes were fixed on the dark water, the rhythmic splashing of the paddles mesmerizing them, as they sat on the awkward raft.

7. Juan thought about these things and he thought about the girl with the dark hair and radiant blue eyes who was now in Miami.

8. A pair of terns circled with intense concentration, one or the other occasionally diving into the warm, silky water near the raft.

9. Two burly arms shook Juan awake. "How far have we come?" asked a groggy voice behind him.

10. Raúl was sitting on the inner tube lashed behind Juan's. He was leaning back now, looking at the feathery clouds.

Student Essay

After considerable deliberation, Ana Vásquez from the Dominican Republic chose to write about her brother's wedding photograph.

A SPECIAL FEELING
ANA VÁSQUEZ

I have many photos in my collection, but there's one that is particu-   1
larly meaningful. It's the wedding photo of my oldest brother, Angel
Luis. The picture was taken on the day of his wedding at the studio of a
local photographer. My brother's dark hair is combed back and his
mustache is neatly trimmed. He is wearing a tan tuxedo, which he
rented for the occasion. He is hugging his bride, Anna. You can see
some of the intricate lacework on her expensive wedding gown.

Every time I see this picture, it is like going back to March 27, 1992,   2
the day it was taken. I remember that day as if it were yesterday. Why?
That day I came to realize just how much I loved my brother. That
morning when I woke up, for some reason I recalled the time when we
were in elementary school. One day my brother's teacher told him he
had to stay 30 minutes after the bell as punishment for some small in-
fraction. I started to cry. I guess the teacher took pity on the tears of a
nine-year-old, so she let him go home with me.

My brother and I had always been close. On the day of the wedding   3
I wondered how our relationship would change. I was excited, but
when the time came for me to get dressed, I started to cry. My cheeks
were wet with tears full of meaning. My mother and my cousin asked
me why I was crying, but I couldn't tell them. I was too deep in thought
and feeling to speak.

I recalled a time back in the Dominican Republic. My brother was   4
teaching me how to ride on a motorcycle. We almost crashed against a
house. He jumped up to see if I was all right. Fortunately, nothing had
happened. But I remember the look of alarm and concern in his face.

I managed to stop crying. It was time to go to the beauty parlor.   5
There, while the beautician was combing my hair, I started to think
about my other brother, who was back home in my country. He
couldn't be with us at the wedding. I broke down again. The beauty
parlor called my mother so she could make me a special Dominican tea
used when someone is upset. They thought I was nervous; but it wasn't

exactly that. I remember my cousins telling me, "Gee, Ana, why are you so nervous? It's not you who is getting married. Imagine how you'll be on your wedding day." I don't think that anybody could guess why I was so sad. I felt that I was losing my brother. It was as if he were leaving home forever. I loved him so much, and the thought of his leaving was hard for me to handle.

I look at the picture again. The two of them are smiling against the 6 dark background. Did Angel know what was going through my mind and my heart that day? I chuckled when I recalled thinking that day that it must have been more than coincidence that Angel had chosen a woman with the same name as my own, even if she did spell it with double *n*.

When my brother was getting dressed, I went to his room. He was 7 playing a tape of Fernandito Villalona, a famous Dominican musician. It was the song that our other brother back home liked most. At that moment he called the Dominican Republic. The two brothers started to talk. I saw my brother's eyes were watery and soon tears were rolling down his cheeks. He hung up the phone. I was crying, too. We looked at each other and hugged each other tight. We didn't speak, but at that moment I felt the love we had for each other.

The picture of Angel and Anna sits on top of the bureau in my bed- 8 room in a simple plastic frame. Now and then I look at them and am reminded how a brother and sister can love each other even if they don't show it every day. Happily, I now see that I was wrong for fearing that I was going to lose my brother. I haven't; instead I have gained a lovely sister.

. . . .

RESPONSE AND ANALYSIS

1. Do you have a married sibling? If so, how has your relationship changed since your brother or sister married?

2. In addition to providing a description of the wedding photograph, Ana narrates several anecdotes and explores her feelings and thoughts about her relationship with her brother and his upcoming marriage. Make three categories: *description, narration, feelings*. List the specific details that Ana has provided in the appropriate category.

3. In paragraph 3, Ana has used a lovely phrase, "tears full of meaning." What does this phrase communicate to you?

Focus on Writing: Explaining References

In paragraph 5 of Ana's essay, she refers to a special Dominican tea and explains that the tea is "used when someone is upset." Ana explains the reference to the tea because she realizes that her audience might not be familiar with this. If Ana had been writing exclusively for a Dominican audience, she might have assumed that the use of the tea for its calming effects was *shared knowledge,* making the explanation unnecessary. However, because she knows that her audience will include those outside her immediate social and ethnic background, Ana provides the explanation. Similarly, in paragraph 7, when she makes a reference to the music of Fernandito Villalona, she explains that he is "a famous Dominican singer."

As you have seen in some of the other readings, writers often make historical and cultural references without explaining them. Ultimately, each writer must decide what may or may not be shared knowledge and when it is necessary to provide further explanation of a reference. For example, if you mention Coca-Cola in your essay, it is probably unnecessary to add "a popular soft drink." Coke has become so familiar throughout the world you can assume that no explanation is necessary. A reference to Coke will be understood by all people who read your essay. But if you mention *hummus,* you will probably want to add that it is a food made from chickpeas eaten throughout the Mideast.

1. Go back to the other student essays you have read. Identify places where the writer has provided an explanation of a reference that might have been unfamiliar to the audience.

2. For further practice, go back to the essays you have written. Revise any essay that you feel could be made more effective by providing an explanation for an unexplained reference.

Focus on Writing: Starting Over

An old saying in English warns against throwing good money after bad—meaning when something is in such poor condition, it doesn't pay to continuously invest in fixing it. You may confront a similar situation with your writing. You invest time generating and organizing ideas and you write the first draft; however, no matter how much revision you do, your writing fails to meet your standards. At this point, you may choose to start the process over rather than continue to work on your original material. This is not a decision you should make too quickly. After all, you may already have put in considerable time and effort. Moreover, you have seen how much can be accomplished with the appropriate revision. Nevertheless, there are times when you might consider taking this step.

When Ana Vásquez was given the assignment to describe a personal photograph of particular significance to her, she immediately thought of a picture of her newborn nephew. She proudly showed the picture of the baby to her classmates. But despite spending some time on the essay, even revising it a number of times, Ana felt that she was not satisfied with it and decided to start over. Let's look at the essay. Afterward you will be able to consider why she may have come to her decision.

PHOTO DESCRIPTION

(First Version)

ANA VÁSQUEZ

This is my nephew Ricky, my brother Angel's first child and my first 1
nephew. This picture was taken almost a month after his birth. Ricky is lying down in his small bed; next to him is a brown teddy bear that is almost as big as he is. The little baby is wearing a diaper and a light blue shirt. He is looking at his proud parents.

Ricky is really important to my whole family and his mother's family, 2
too. He is the first member of my family to be born in the United States, a Dominican American. Besides that, he is my parents' first grandson. He is also the first grandchild of his mother's parents. So for both sides he is the center of attention and the source of happiness.

What sort of man will Ricky be when he grows up? I know my par- 3
ents are worried that he won't speak Spanish. Angel married the daughter of Italian immigrants. Because of her Italian, she can understand some Spanish fairly well, but she doesn't speak it. My brother and sister-in-law do not speak Spanish at home. I wonder if my mother and father will eventually learn English. I look at the picture.

While my sister-in-law was pregnant, I didn't realize the baby would 4
mean so much to me. I remember how I melted the first time I saw him at the hospital. Ricky, you are my first nephew and I love you very much.

· · · · · · · · · · · · · · · · ·

ANALYSIS

1. Do you find Ana's essay successful? Bring specific evidence to support your opinion.

2. Try to make some suggestions on ways Ana could have made the essay more successful had she continued working on it.

Ana's decision to begin again meant that she would start the writing process over—generating ideas, writing the first draft, and revising. Now let's look at the early draft of the essay you read earlier. Afterward you will be able to analyze the changes that Ana made as she revised the essay.

A SPECIAL FEELING

(Early Draft)

ANA VÁSQUEZ

I have many photos in my collection but there's one that is very special to me. It's a photo of my oldest brother's wedding. In this photo his wife is hugging him and he's hugging her.   1

Every time I see this picture, it's like going back to March 27, 1992, the day it was taken. I remember that day as if it was today. Why? That day was when I realized how much I loved my brother. My brother and I were never separated from each other. We had lived together until the time he decided to get married.   2

It was March 27, 1992 in the morning. I was a little excited about the wedding but when the time came for me to get dressed, I started to cry. I couldn't stop. My cheeks were wet with tears full of meaning. My mother and my cousins asked me why I was crying. I couldn't tell them. All I did was cry and cry.   3

I stopped for awhile and I went to the beauty parlor. There, as the woman was combing my hair, I started to cry again. The woman called my house so my mother could make me tea. After the beauty parlor, I went home and drank the tea and calmed down.   4

Nobody knew why I was so sad. I felt that I was losing my brother. It was like he was going to leave home forever. I loved him so much and I wanted him to stay with us.   5

This was the first wedding in my family and my other brother wasn't here. They were in my country so they couldn't be with us on this important occasion.   6

When my brother was getting dressed, I went to his room. He had a   7
tape that reminded us of our brother back home. Tears appeared on his
cheek. Of course, tears were running down my cheeks. We hugged
each other really tight. Although we couldn't talk, I felt at that moment
the love we had for each other. I thought about how much the three of
us—my two brothers and I—love each other.

This picture is always going to remind me of how much a brother   8
and a sister could love each other even if they don't show it every day.
Since this picture was taken, time has made me see that I was wrong to
think that I was going to lose my brother. Instead I won a lovely sister.

. . . .

ANALYSIS

1. Reread the revised essay. Make a list of the changes Ana has made and explain why
   you think she made them. Use these terms to help your analysis: *anecdote, description,* and *explanation of references.*

2. In addition, Ana changed some of the wording in the final version of her essay.
   List these changes and explain why you think each was made.

Essay Writing

. . . .

GENERATING IDEAS

Freewrite about a photograph from your personal collection. You may want to use
the categories below as a guide, but feel free to consider anything related to the
topic.

a. Where and when was the photograph taken?

b. Who appears in the photograph?

c. Provide a description of the photograph, including such details as the background, what the people in the photo are doing, etc.

d. Add a detail not yet mentioned about the photograph.

e. What was happening in the lives of the people when the photograph was taken?

f. What else does the photograph remind you of?

g. Why is this photograph particularly meaningful to you?

h. How do you feel about the people and places of the photograph today, months or years after it was taken? Has anything changed in your life or in the lives of those in the photograph?

· · · · · · · · · · · · · · · · ·

ASSIGNMENT

Use your freewriting as the basis for an essay describing a meaningful photograph you have. Keep in mind the elements that Ana has included in her successful essay: in addition to describing the photo, she narrates a number of anecdotes she associates with the picture. Be sure to provide an explanation for any references that might not be familiar to your audience. Also, if your first choice doesn't work out to your satisfaction, as in Ana's case, don't be reluctant to choose a different photograph and start over. After you have written an early draft of your essay, share it with a teacher or a friend and explore possible revisions that would make it even more successful.

8

FRIENDS AND FAMILY

. . . .

The reading and writing activities in this chapter focus on the theme of personal re-lationships. Have you been fortunate enough to maintain close ties with friends and family in your homeland and to develop new ones here in the United States?

READING FROM

My Ántonia

WILLA CATHER

. . . .

ESTABLISHING THE CONTEXT

As was the case with many of the nations of Europe, immigration to the United States from the Czech homeland reached its peak generations ago. From the middle of the nineteenth century until the start of World War I, more than 3 million Czechs came to the United States, the majority settling in the urban centers of the midwest or building farms on the *Great Plains* or *prairie,* the wide stretch of flat grassy land in the heart of the North American continent. After World War II, Czech immigra-tion to the United States was revived as thousands of refugees from wartorn Europe made their way to America. Then in 1968, thousands of Czechs fled their homeland when the Soviet Union invaded to crush their nation's growing movement toward democracy.

Willa Cather was raised in rural Nebraska among the immigrants who had come from Sweden, Russia, Germany, and Bohemia—a major region in the Czech Repub-lic—to work the land of the American continent. In this excerpt from *My Ántonia,* the Burdens, an established farming family in the region, pay a visit to their new Czech neighbors. The visit marks the beginning of a friendship between two chil-dren: Jim Burden, born and raised in the United States, and Ántonia Shimerda, who has just come with her family from Bohemia.

. . . .

TO BEGIN

1. Do you have friends and acquaintances outside your immediate ethnic group? What issues, if any, have arisen because you come from different backgrounds?

2. Read the first paragraph of the selection. What can you infer about the way the Shimerdas have been living? Later as you continue reading, notice the many de-tails that reveal the way of life of these immigrant pioneers.

3. You will probably come across some unfamiliar words in this excerpt from *My Ántonia*. Sometimes it helps to familiarize yourself with key vocabulary before you begin reading. The underlined words in the following passages are all related to the way of life of the Bohemian settlers. Try to determine the meaning of each word by its context. Then provide a dictionary definition either in English or in your native language.

   a. The Bohemian family, grandmother told me as we drove along, had bought the homestead of a fellow countryman, Peter Krajiek, and had paid him more than it was worth.

   b. "It's no better than a badger hole; no proper dugout at all."

   c. Presently, against one of those banks, I saw a sort of shed, thatched with the same wine-colored grass that grew everywhere.

There will probably be other unfamiliar words in this excerpt. Remember, however, that you can still enjoy and understand what you read without knowing the definition of every word. Try to use the context to guess at the unfamiliar words and phrases as you read for your interest and pleasure about the visit between the Burdens and the Shimerdas. Don't be overly concerned with words and phrases you don't understand; there will be another vocabulary activity to do after you read, respond to, and analyze the selection.

FROM

MY ÁNTONIA

WILLA CATHER

On Sunday morning Otto Fuchs was to drive us over to make the acquaintance of our new Bohemian neighbors. We were taking them some provisions, as they had come to live on a wild place where there was no garden or chicken-house, and very little broken land. Fuchs brought up a sack of potatoes and a piece of cured pork from the cellar, and grandmother packed some loaves of Saturday's bread, a jar of butter, and several pumpkin pies in the straw of the wagon-box. We clambered up to the front seat and jolted off past the little pond and along the road that climbed to the big cornfield.

I could hardly wait to to see what lay beyond that cornfield; but there was only red grass like ours, and nothing else, though from the high wagon-seat one could look off a long way. The road ran about like a wild thing, avoiding the deep draws, crossing them where they were wide and shallow. And all along it, wherever it looped or ran, the sunflowers grew; some of them were as big as little trees, with great rough leaves and many branches which bore dozens of blossoms. They made a gold ribbon across the prairie. Occasionally one of the horses would tear off with his teeth a plant full of blossoms, and walk along munching it, the flowers nodding in time to his bites as he ate down toward them.

The Bohemian family, grandmother told me as we drove along, had 3 bought the homestead of a fellow countryman, Peter Krajiek, and had paid him more than it was worth. Their agreement with him was made before they left the old country, through a cousin of his, who was also a relative of Mrs. Shimerda. The Shimerdas were the first Bohemian family to come to this part of the country. Krajiek was their only interpreter, and could tell them anything he chose. They could not speak enough English to ask for advice, or even or make their most pressing wants known. One son, Fuchs said, was well-grown, and strong enough to work the land; but the father was old and frail and knew nothing about farming. He was a weaver by trade; had been a skilled workman on tapestries and upholstery materials. He had brought his fiddle with him, which wouldn't be of much use here, though he used to pick up money by it at home.

"If they're nice people, I hate to think of them spending the winter in 4 that cave of Krajiek's," said grandmother. "It's no better than a badger hole; no proper dugout at all. And I hear he's made them pay twenty dollars for his old cookstove that ain't worth ten."

"Yes'm," said Otto; "and he's sold 'em his oxen and his two bony old 5 horses for the price of good workteams. I'd have interfered about the horses—the old man can understand some German—if I'd 'a' thought it would do any good. But Bohemians has a natural distrust of Austrians."

Grandmother looked interested. "Now, why is that, Otto?" 6

Fuchs wrinkled his brow and nose. "Well, ma'm, it's politics. It 7 would take me a long while to explain."

The land was growing rougher; I was told that we were approaching 8 Squaw Creek, which cut up the west half of the Shimerdas' place and made the land of little value for farming. Soon we could see the broken, grassy clay cliffs which indicated the windings of the stream, and the glittering tops of the cottonwoods and ash trees that grew down in the ravine. Some of the cottonwoods had already turned, and the yellow leaves and shining white bark made them look like the gold and silver trees in fairy tales.

As we approached the Shimerdas' dwelling, I could still see nothing   9
but rough red hillocks, and draws with shelving banks and long roots
hanging out where the earth had crumbled away. Presently, against one
of those banks, I saw a sort of shed, thatched with the same wine-
colored grass that grew everywhere. Near it tilted a shattered windmill
frame, that had no wheel. We drove up to this skeleton to tie our horses,
and then I saw a door and window sunk deep in the drawbank. The
door stood open, and a woman and a girl of fourteen ran out and
looked up at us hopefully. A little girl trailed along behind them. The
woman had on her head the same embroidered shawl with silk fringes
that she wore when she had alighted from the train at Black Hawk. She
was not old, but she was certainly not young. Her face was alert and
lively, with a sharp chin and shrewd little eyes. She shook grandmother's hand energetically.

"Very glad, very glad!" she ejaculated. Immediately she pointed to   10
the bank out of which she had emerged and said, 'House no good,
house no good!'

Grandmother nodded consolingly. "You'll get fixed up comfortable   11
after while, Mrs. Shimerda; make good house."

My grandmother always spoke in a very loud tone to foreigners, as if   12
they were deaf. She made Mrs. Shimerda understand the friendly inten-
tion of our visit, and the Bohemian woman handled the loaves of bread
and even smelled them, and examined the pies with lively curiosity, ex-
claiming, "Much good, much thank!"—and again she wrung grandmother's hand.

The oldest son, Ambroz—they called it Ambrosch—came out of the   13
cave and stood beside his mother. He was nineteen years old, short and
broad-backed, with a close-cropped, flat head, and a wide, flat face.
His hazel eyes were little and shrewd, like his mother's, but more shy
and suspicious; they fairly snapped at the food. The family had been living on corncakes and sorghum molasses for three days.

The little girl was pretty, but Án-tonia—they accented the name thus,   14
strongly, when they spoke to her—was still prettier. I remembered what
the conductor had said about her eyes. They were big and warm and
full of light, like the sun shining on brown pools in the wood. Her skin
was brown, too, and in her cheeks she had a glow of rich, dark color.
Her brown hair was curly and wild-looking. The little sister, whom they
called Yulka (Julka), was fair, and seemed mild and obedient. While I
stood awkwardly confronting the two girls, Krajiek came up from the
barn to see what was going on. With him was another Shimerda son.

Even from a distance one could see that there was something strange about this boy. As he approached us, he began to make uncouth noises, and held up his hands to show us his fingers, which were webbed to the first knuckle, like a duck's foot. When he saw me draw back, he began to crow delightedly, "Hoo, hoo-hoo, hoo-hoo!" like a rooster. His mother scowled and said sternly, "Marek!" then spoke rapidly to Krajiek in Bohemian.

"She wants me to tell you he won't hurt nobody, Mrs. Burden. He   15
was born like that. The others are smart. Ambrosch, he make good farmer." He struck Ambrosch on the back, and the boy smiled knowingly.

At that moment the father came out of the hole in the bank. He wore   16
no hat, and his thick, iron-grey hair was brushed straight back from his forehead. It was so long that it bushed out behind his ears, and made him look like the old portraits I remembered in Virginia. He was tall and slender, and his thin shoulders stooped. He looked at us understandingly, then took grandmother's hand and bent over it. I noticed how white and well-shaped his own hands were. They looked calm, somehow, and skilled. His eyes were melancholy, and were set back deep under his brow. His face was ruggedly formed, but it looked like ashes—like something from which all the warmth and light had died out. Everything about this old man was in keeping with his dignified manner. He was neatly dressed. Under his coat he wore a knitted grey vest, and, instead of a collar, a silk scarf of a dark bronze-green, carefully crossed and held together by a red coral pin. While Krajiek was translating for Mr. Shimerda, Ántonia came up to me and held out her hand coaxingly. In a moment we were running up the steep drawside together, Yulka trotting after us.

When we reached the level and could see the gold tree-tops, I   17
pointed toward them, and Ántonia laughed and squeezed my hand as if to tell me how glad she was I had come. We raced off toward Squaw Creek and did not stop until the ground itself stopped—fell away before us so abruptly that the next step would have been out into the tree-tops. We stood panting on the edge of the ravine, looking down at the trees and bushes that grew below us. The wind was so strong that I had to hold my hat on, and the girls' skirts were blown out before them. Ántonia seemed to like it; she held her little sister by the hand and chattered away in that language which seemed to me spoken so much more rapidly than mine. She looked at me, her eyes fairly blazing with things she could not say.

"Name? What name?" she asked, touching me on the shoulder. I told   18
her my name, and she repeated it after me and made Yulka say it. She
pointed into the gold cottonwood tree behind whose top we stood and
said again, "What name?"

We sat down and made a nest in the long red grass. Yulka curled   19
up like a baby rabbit and played with a grasshopper. Ántonia pointed
up to the sky and questioned me with her glance. I gave her the word,
but she was not satisfied and pointed to my eyes. I told her, and she
repeated the word, making it sound like "ice." She pointed up to the
sky, then to my eyes, then back to the sky, with movements so quick
and impulsive that she distracted me, and I had no idea what she
wanted. She got up on her knees and wrung her hands. She pointed to
her own eyes and shook her head, then to mine and to the sky, nodding violently.

"Oh," I exclaimed, "blue; blue sky."   20

She clapped her hands and murmured, "Blue sky, blue eyes," as if it   21
amused her. While we snuggled down there out of the wind, she
learned a score of words. She was quick, and very eager. We were so
deep in the grass that we could see nothing but the blue sky over us and
the gold tree in front of us. It was wonderfully pleasant. After Ántonia
had said the new words over and over, she wanted to give me a little
chased silver ring she wore on her middle finger. When she coaxed and
insisted, I repulsed her quite sternly. I didn't want her ring, and I felt
there was something reckless and extravagant about her wishing to give
it away to a boy she had never seen before. No wonder Krajiek got the
better of these people, if this was how they behaved.

While we were disputing about the ring, I heard a mournful voice   22
calling, "Án-tonia, Án-tonia!" She sprang up like a hare. "*Tatinek!*
Tatinek!" she shouted, and we ran to meet the old man who was coming toward us. Ántonia reached him first, took his hand and kissed it.
When I came up, he touched my shoulder and looked searchingly
down into my face for several seconds. I became somewhat
embarrassed, for I was used to being taken for granted by my
elders.

We went with Mr. Shimerda back to the dugout, where grandmother   23
was waiting for me. Before I got into the wagon, he took a book out of
his pocket, opened it, and showed me a page with two alphabets, one
English and the other Bohemian. He placed this book in my grandmother's hands, looked at her entreatingly, and said, with an earnest-
ness which I shall never forget, "Te-e-ach, te-e-ach my Án-tonia!"

· · · · · · · · · · · · · · · · ·

RESPONSE AND ANALYSIS

1. Write for a few minutes in response to what you have read. Besides summarizing, you may want to explore your feelings and thoughts about the reading. It may be helpful to consider these categories:

   a. what you understood about the reading

   b. something that puzzled you in the reading

   c. something you would like to discuss with the writer or one of the characters

   d. a memory the reading evoked

   e. how you felt about the reading

2. A number of characters are mentioned in the reading. Use the context of the story to identify each:

   a. the narrator

   b. Peter Krajiek

   c. Otto

   d. Ambrosch

   e. Yulka

   f. Marek

   g. Mrs. Burden

   h. Ántonia

3. What else have you learned about the living conditions of the Bohemian settlers on the prairie? Bring specific evidence from the text to support your answer.

4. The second paragraph of the reading begins, "I could hardly wait to see what lay beyond that cornfield; but there was only red grass like ours, and nothing else, though from the high wagon-seat one could look off a long way." An important theme in the reading is the setting, established by the many details providing the physical description of the prairie. What sort of picture do you have of the region? Without looking back at the text, try to write a paragraph describing the prairie in the times of the pioneers, as you imagine it based on the description provided in *My Ántonia*.

5. Another theme in the reading concerns the limited English of the immigrants. List the specific instances where this theme is explored.

6. By the end, it is apparent that a friendship is developing between Ántonia and the Burden boy. Try to anticipate how this relationship may develop in the future.

. . . .

FURTHER EXPLORATION OF LANGUAGE AND LITERATURE: DIALECTS OF ENGLISH

You are already familiar with the term *dialogue,* the words spoken by the characters in a story. The way we speak is influenced by several factors: the geographical region we come from, our social status, income level, and the number of years in school. In addition, most of us adapt the way we speak to fit the situation of the moment. You probably wouldn't speak the same way with your parents, in school, or on a job interview as you would "hanging out" with your friends. The term *dialect* refers to a different variety or way of speaking the same language.

Effective dialogue captures the particular dialect of the character. For example, look at Mrs. Burden's comment about the farm the Shimerdas have bought:

"It's no better than a badger hole; no proper dugout at all. And I hear he's made them pay twenty dollars for his old cookstove that ain't worth ten."

Mrs. Burden has used the word *ain't.* This construction, part of her dialect, is usually considered non-standard English—that is, not acceptable in formal situations such as in school or on a job interview. In *standard* English—the language used in formal situations—the equivalent of *it ain't* would be *it isn't.* To capture the old woman's informal conversation with her employee, Otto, the non-standard construction is used.

Sometimes you will find dialogue written not in the standard spelling but in a way that imitates how the words are pronounced, a technique known as *dialect spelling.* For example, look at Otto's response to Mrs. Burden's comment:

"Yes'm," said Otto; "and he's sold 'em his oxen and his two bony old horses for the price of good workteams. I'd have interfered about the horses—the old man can understand some German—if I'd 'a' thought it would do any good. . . . "

In standard English spelling, *yes'm* would be *yes, madam* or *yes, ma'am.* To capture the way the character actually speaks, the dialect spelling is used. Similarly, notice the comment "he's sold 'em." Of course, the standard English spelling would be *he's sold them* or *he has sold them.* Otto later adds that he would have interfered, "if I'd 'a' thought it would do any good." Can you figure out how to write this last phrase in standard English spelling?

Naturally, you would expect the English of the newly arrived immigrants to be characterized by constructions outside of standard English. Because of Mrs. Shimerda's limited English, she is unable to say, "The house we must live in is not good." Instead she says simply, "House no good, house no good." Throughout the reading, the speech of the Shimerdas reveals their limited English. For each piece of dialogue that follows, written in the dialect of the Czech immigrants, try to determine an appropriate standard English equivalent.

a. Very glad, very glad.

b. Much good, much thank.

c. Name? What name?

d. Blue sky, blue eyes.

e. Te-e-ach, te-e-ach my Ántonia!

. . . .

VOCABULARY

In the following passages, try to determine the meaning of each underlined word by its context. (You may want to choose additional words from the reading if you found the vocabulary very challenging.) Then provide a dictionary definition, either in English or in your native language. Finally, read the excerpt from *My Ántonia* a second time, paying closer attention to the words you have learned as well as the other points discussed in the previous activities.

1. We were taking them some <u>provisions,</u> as they had come to live on a wild place where there was no garden or chicken-house, and very little broken land.

2. Occasionally one of the horses would tear off with his teeth a plant full of blossoms, and walk along <u>munching</u> it, the flowers <u>nodding</u> in time to his bites as he ate down toward them.

3. He was a <u>weaver</u> by trade; had been a skilled workman on <u>tapestries</u> and <u>upholstery</u> materials.

4. As we approached the Shimerdas' <u>dwelling,</u> I could still see nothing . . .

5. His mother <u>scowled</u> and said <u>sternly,</u> "Marek!" then spoke rapidly to Krajiek in Bohemian.

6. His eyes were <u>melancholy,</u> and were set back deep under his brow.

7. We stood <u>panting</u> at the edge of the <u>ravine,</u> looking down at the trees and bushes that grew below us.

8. When she <u>coaxed</u> and insisted, I <u>repulsed</u> her quite sternly.

9. I didn't want her ring, and I felt there was something <u>reckless</u> and <u>extravagant</u> about her wishing to give it away to a boy she had never seen before.

10. He placed this book in my grandmother's hands, looked at her <u>entreatingly,</u> and said, with an <u>earnestness</u> which I shall never forget, "Te-e-ach, te-e-ach my Án-tonia!"

Student Essay

When asked to describe a friend, Addys Reynoso thought of a special relationship she had had in her childhood in the Dominican Republic. Although she knew Jochy for a short time, the memories remain.

JOCHY

ADDYS REYNOSO

I remember the summer day when my cousin Amalfi showed me her new friend Jochy. Through his curly brown hair I saw two bright eyes shining like the stars over the beaches of Santo Domingo. He was so tiny and cute, how could you not fall in love with him? Jochy soon became my special friend.   1

For the next few weeks Jochy used to run away from my cousin's house next door. We would spend hours and hours playing. My mother would often get angry as Jochy and I would jump on the beds and run from one side of the house to the other, knocking down pots and pans, toys, pillows, anything that got in our way. I was seven years old at the time.   2

One day Jochy and I got lost on my grandfather's property. My grandfather owned hundreds of acres of land that had once been part of a large sugar plantation. He always talked about farming but to this day the land sits as it did when I was a child: a large expanse of thick tropical plants with fruit trees: mangos, bananas, coconut palms, and guavas. I had never walked on the land alone without the supervision of an adult. I held Jochy in my arms and walked with him for hours. Using a large palm tree as a starting point, we walked in different directions, always coming back to that tree. I was so scared but Jochy was indifferent. He couldn't understand what was going on. He just moved his head from side to side. Finally we chose the right direction from the tree and we got to the house. My grandmother asked, "Where have you been?" I just answered, "Playing with Jochy." Jochy wandered out of the house.   3

Even though Jochy couldn't speak with words, his eyes were eloquent. Once he came to my house as we were eating dinner. Jochy was so anxious as he moved from one side to another making strange noises. I didn't understand: what was he trying to tell me? I stood up to investigate and   4 went outside. Maybe something was going on. I didn't notice anything unusual. When I came back I found Jochy eating my dinner! "Of course," I thought, "He was trying to tell me he was hungry."

They say, "Easy come, easy go," but saying goodbye to Jochy was 5 probably the most difficult thing I had to do to that point in my life. One morning I went to my cousin's house to see Jochy. His bright eyes had become dim. He looked up at me with sad eyes and started to bark as if to say, "It's been a wonderful couple of weeks." Jochy was dying and there was nothing I could do. The veterinarian said it would be a matter of days. Soon after that my friend died, leaving me with tears and memories that still come back to me years later.

People say that a dog is a man's best friend. A dog was this young 6 girl's best friend, too.

. . . .

RESPONSE AND ANALYSIS

1. Were you surprised to learn that Addys's friend Jochy was a dog? Did Addys give you any clue early in the essay that she was not referring to a person?

2. Identify and explain the simile that Addys uses to describe Jochy's eyes. Where else in the essay are the eyes mentioned?

3. Notice that the body of Addys's essay is organized into paragraphs on a specific theme. What themes are developed in paragraphs 2 through 5? For each theme, identify the topic sentence.

4. What does the conclusion add to the essay?

READING FROM

Mount Allegro

JERRE MANGIONE

. . . .

ESTABLISHING THE CONTEXT

Between 1880 and 1920 more than 4 million Italians immigrated to the United States. Unlike many European immigrants in those days, however, it was quite common for Italian men to come here to work for a short time, earn money, and return home with their savings. In fact, almost one-half of the Italian immigrants during those years were so-called *birds of paradise*. They usually returned to Italy after a stay in the United States, often making the journey several times during their lifetime. Those who remained established large communities in the cities of the Northeast, as well as in Chicago and San Francisco.

The elimination in 1965 of regulations that had favored immigrants from northern Europe resulted in increased immigration from Asia, Africa, and the Americas, dramatically changing the character of the American population. It also benefited Italians and the other peoples of southern Europe. In the decade following the passing of the Immigration and Nationality Act of 1965, more than a quarter-million Italians immigrated to the United States. Although this number has dropped substantially in the past two decades, thousands of Italians continue to come to live in the United States each year, both legally and illegally. In fact, it has been estimated that Italians who overstay their tourist visas comprise the largest group of illegal aliens in New York City today.

In *Mount Allegro: A Memoir of Italian American Life*, Jerre Mangione describes his childhood in a working-class Italian neighborhood of Rochester, New York, in the 1920s. In the following excerpt, Mangione recalls his father, Don Peppino, an immigrant from Sicily (an island off the southern coast of Italy).

. . . .

TO BEGIN

Read the first sentence of the selection: "There was a banquet for as many occasions as my father could imagine. . . . " A *banquet* is a dinner in celebration of a special person or occasion. What sort of occasions call for a banquet in your culture? What kinds of foods are served? How else is the occasion celebrated? After you complete the reading, you will be able to compare the banquets you are familiar with to those typical of the Sicilian American immigrants several generations ago.

You will probably come across some unfamiliar words in this excerpt from *Mount Allegro*. Remember, however, that you can still enjoy and understand what you read without knowing the definition of every word. Try to use the context to guess at the unfamiliar words and phrases as you read for your interest and pleasure a son's description of his Sicilian father. Don't be overly concerned with words and phrases you don't understand; there will be a vocabulary activity to do after you read, respond to, and analyze the selection.

FROM

Mount Allegro

JERRE MANGIONE

There was a banquet for as many occasions as my father could imagine, and his imagination was fertile. He once gave a banquet for some relatives who were moving to California and, when they were suddenly obliged to change their plans, he gave another banquet to celebrate their staying. He no sooner had finished with one banquet than he began to talk about the next one. He had the pride of an artist in his cooking, particularly his pastrymaking, and he never denied the story that when the Baron Michele, the richest man in the province of Girgenti, went on his honeymoon to Palermo, he took my father along to prepare his favorite desserts.

He was especially noted for a Sicilian delicacy called *cannolo*, which was unsurpassed by any of the other pastrycooks in Rochester and seldom equaled even in New York and Palermo. As a boy he had been apprenticed to a famous Sicilian pastrycook and he learned his trade well. He might have become a celebrated pastrymaker had he remained in Sicily, but here in America, the land of ice cream and pie, there was not enough of a market for his products and he became another factory worker, expressing his real talents on holidays and other occasions when he could give banquets for his friends and relatives.

Although his *cannoli* were masterpieces, his recipe for making them was no secret and he willingly itemized it for anyone who wanted to attempt it. Needless to say, no one ever approached his results, though several of his more determined imitators came to his kitchen to watch every move and measurement he made. The ingredients were simple: cottage cheese refined to a smooth paste; tiny bits of chocolate mixed into the paste, and a few drops of a magical spirit known as *cannela* (a liquid cinnamon), whose sharp odor recurs to me with fully as many memories as a cup of tea ever gave Proust. The trick, my father claimed, was not so much in concocting the cream as in preparing the crisp, cylindrical shells that held it.

Like most good art, the *cannoli* looked simple but entailed much more work than would seem necessary to a layman. So that he would have no distractions, my father often started making his *cannoli* at three in the morning. Until dawn, he hovered over the shells like an anxious mother, nursing them to their proper crispness. After the shells were done, there were almonds to be roasted and crushed into golden crumbs that would be sprinkled over the ends of the *cannoli* once they were filled with cream. And always there had to be perfect timing. Judging from the amount of patience *cannoli* required and the small amount my father usually showed, he must have saved a little patience every day so that he would have enough to make his *cannoli* once or twice a year.

The more enthusiasts his *cannoli* bred, the less inclined he was to make them. His explanation was that since he did not have time to make *cannoli* for all his friends and relatives, he would make them for no one but his immediate family. When occasionally he broke this rule, our house would take on the atmosphere of a secret underground society.   5

My father would solemnly warn us not to tell anyone he was making *cannoli* and, when they were finished, he would count them out carefully into empty shoe-boxes he hoarded for such occasions and sneak them to favored relatives and friends, the right number for each family, begging them not to say a word about the gift to anyone lest someone take offense at being left out.   6

He never took money for his *cannoli* and would be hurt if anyone tried to pay him. Once he opened a pastry shop and featured *cannoli* as his specialty. For a few months business seemed good; many Sicilians bought many *cannoli*. Yet my father made no money. It was not until he closed the shop that he realized he had failed to charge enough to cover the cost of the ingredients.   7

In those few months he was in business scores of new *cannoli* addicts were born and, ever afterward, they telephoned hopefully a week before an important holiday like Christmas or Easter to ask if Don Peppino would make a few dozen *cannoli* for them. He enjoyed answering the telephone at such times, even though his answer was usually No, for like any good artist it heartened him to know that his product was still appreciated and in demand.   8

As temperamental as he was, my father could be relied on to assume responsibility for cooking all Sunday dinners. This sometimes involved preparing at least a half-dozen courses for as many as twenty persons. To show her gratitude, my mother gladly took charge of such details as serving and dishwashing and, when she was certain there were enough guests listening, she complimented him extravagantly not only on his abilities as a cook but also as a carpenter and a paperhanger.   9

We were all aware of the strategy behind her flattery, yet we realized   10 that she sincerely believed him to be the best cook on earth. When they teased each other, my mother would declare that it was only because of his cooking skill that she had married him, whereupon my father would retort that she could be sure that was not the reason he had married her.

On Sunday mornings he rose earlier than the rest of us and took 11 complete charge of the kitchen, using my mother and one of the children for the menial jobs of peeling, grating, and slicing. His meals had an extravagance about them that was far out of proportion to his salary. To finance them he often had to borrow money. But for him that was less important than sharing the joy and warmth that good food and gay company created.

Like the rest of my relatives, he believed implicitly in the goodness of 12 food and liked to repeat the motto: "Food is the only thing you can take with you when you die." This was not said in any morbid sense, but as encouragement for more eating. If a guest had the temerity to turn down another helping of food, the motto was sprung on him with great gusto if it was obvious that the guest's eating capacity had not yet reached its limits (the guest, of course, was never permitted to decide for himself what those limits might be), and as a polite rebuke if it was clear to the host that his guest could not eat another morsel of food without bursting. My relatives' passionate faith in food as a soul and body builder was, in the last analysis, an expression of their philosophy: If you ate well, you felt well. And if you felt well, all was well with the world.

For weekday suppers a soup course, some spaghetti and meat, fol- 13 lowed by a salad, was an ample meal. But on Sundays and holidays it was assumed that your appetite became gargantuan and, besides soup and salad, you were expected to stow away at least three different courses of meat, four or five vegetables, along with celery and fennel, all topped off with pastry, fruits, and nuts.

. . .

My father was a powerhouse of charm. No matter how engrossed his 14 guests might be in his cookery or how loudly they might be babbling to each other, when he rose from his chair he had their complete attention. His opening words at the table were part of his own ritual.

"It is terribly dark," he would say, even though the sun might be 15 streaming into the room. "We must light the candles." Thereupon he would pour red wine into the tumbler of each guest.

With each successive "lighting of the candles" the room would glow 16 more and more with the good cheer of the guests. The meal would continue for at least two hours, getting noisier with talk and laughter as the appetites of the guests diminished. By the time the last course was served, the conversation was so loud that it was difficult to be heard unless you had a strong voice. The climax of the meal would be reached with the serving of the vermouth and whatever pastries my father had baked for the occasion.

At that point my father would rise, stand on a chair to make himself [17] taller and wave a bottle to command attention; then, by some miracle which I have never understood, proceed to toast each guest seated at the table in rhyming double-entendres. With each toast, he poured out a drink of the vermouth in a special glass which was shared by all, and handed it to the guest he had toasted. While he waited for the glass to be emptied, he composed the next toast.

Regardless of how many guests there were at the table, my father [18] never seemed to become exhausted or repetitious. Many of the guests he had toasted on other occasions, but he had a different toast for them each time. If the guest was a recent acquaintance, my father's toast was likely to be in the nature of a compliment. For older friends he made up toasts that lampooned their favorite weakness without causing any offense. The older the friend, the franker the toast.

Some of the toasts were in the nature of congratulations for newly ac- [19] quired jobs, triumphs over recent illnesses, and blessed events. Only the suckling infants, who were considered too young to be of drinking age, did not receive individual toasts. When my father was through toasting the adults, he toasted the infants collectively and then poured out a drink for himself.

The dinner usually closed with my Uncle Nino making a speech in [20] pure Italian. He used the longest and most sonorous words he knew and, although only a few of the guests had gone to school long enough to understand everything he said, everyone listened attentively. His speeches either eulogized the occasion and the company present or dealt with some scholastic honor that one of the children had achieved.

Uncle Nino had surprising ideas about what constituted a scholastic [21] honor. If one of us passed a grade or brought home a report card that wasn't littered with failing marks, or happened to mention that his teacher had singled him out to erase the blackboards or to take charge of opening or closing the classroom windows, that was sufficient incentive to launch Uncle Nino into an oration on "scholastic honor" that was never less than a half-hour long.

. . . .

RESPONSE AND ANALYSIS

1. Write for a few minutes in response to what you have read. Besides summarizing, you may want to explore your feelings and thoughts about the story. It may be helpful to consider these categories:

    a. what you understood about the reading

    b. something that puzzled you in the reading

    c. something you would like to discuss with the writer or one of the characters

    d. a memory the reading evoked

    e. how you felt about the reading

2. It is said of Don Peppino that "he had *the pride of an artist* in his cooking, particularly his pastrymaking. . . . " What does this phrase communicate to you? Do you know any people who feel this way about a special skill they have? Explain.

3. Besides his love of preparing food, what other aspects of Don Peppino are explored?

4. Many features typical of a Sicilian American banquet are described in the reading: the food, the loud conversation, the toasts, the closing speech. Without looking back at the text, try to write a paragraph describing the banquets that the people of Mount Allegro enjoyed. How do they compare with the festive meals familiar to you?

5. Like Mr. Shimerda in *My Ántonia,* Don Peppino had been a skilled worker in the old country. Upon immigrating to America, however, both men end up doing manual labor, on a farm or in a factory. Do you know anyone who has had a similar experience? What issues arise when educated professionals or skilled workers are unable to find appropriate employment when they immigrate?

. . . .

FURTHER EXPLORATION OF LANGUAGE AND LITERATURE: MORE ABOUT DIALECTS

At the end of the family banquets, Uncle Nino would make a speech in what is described as "pure Italian." What is "pure Italian?" The answer relates once again to the idea of *dialects,* a concept introduced earlier in this chapter. As you have seen, a dialect is a different variety or way of speaking a particular language; the dialect you speak is usually related to the amount of education you have, your social status in the community, income level, and ethnicity. Another important factor that influences your dialect is the geographical region you come from. The variety of language used by people in one part of a country is usually not identical to that used by people living in a different part of the country. In fact, sometimes regional dialects may be so dissimilar that speakers from different parts of the same country may have difficulty understanding each other.

The people of Mount Allegro come from Sicily, an island off the southern coast of Italy with a regional dialect quite different from standard Italian. Therefore, much is made of Uncle Nino's ability to speak "pure" or standard Italian. In fact, he is probably the only member of the family who is able to speak standard Italian, and this is significant enough to deserve special mention.

1. Are you familiar with the regional dialect differences in the language(s) of your homeland? Discuss some of these.

2. A number of regional dialects are used in the United States. Even if you have not traveled much, you have certainly heard many Americans on television or radio from different parts of the country. Discuss some of the features you may have noticed in the English they use.

. . . .

VOCABULARY

In the following passages, try to determine the meaning of each underlined word by its context. (You may want to choose additional words from the reading if you found the vocabulary very challenging.) Then provide a dictionary definition either in English or in your native language. Finally, read the excerpt from *Mount Allegro* a second time, paying close attention to the new words you have learned as well as the other points discussed in the previous activities.

1. He once gave a banquet for some relatives who were moving to California and, when they were suddenly obliged to change their plans, he gave another banquet to celebrate their staying.

2. As a boy he had been apprenticed to a famous Sicilian pastrycook and he learned his trade well.

3. . . . when they were finished, he would count them out carefully into empty shoe-boxes he hoarded for such occasions and sneak them to favored relatives and friends, the right number for each family. . . .

4. In those few months he was in business scores of new *cannoli* addicts were born. . . .

5. To show her gratitude, my mother gladly took charge of such details as serving and dishwashing and, when she was certain there were enough guests listening, she complimented him extravagantly not only on his abilities as a cook but also as a carpenter and a paperhanger.

6. On Sunday mornings he rose earlier than the rest of us and took complete

charge of the kitchen, using my mother and one of the children for the <u>menial</u> jobs of peeling, grating, and slicing.

7. For weekday suppers a soup course, some spaghetti and meat, followed by a salad, was an <u>ample</u> meal.

8. But on Sundays and holidays it was assumed that your appetite became <u>gargantuan</u> and, besides soup and salad, you were expected to <u>stow away</u> at least three different courses of meat, four or five vegetables, along with celery and fennel, all topped off with pastry, fruits, and nuts.

9. No matter how <u>engrossed</u> his guests might be in his cookery or how loudly they might be <u>babbling</u> to each other, when he rose from his chair he had their complete attention.

10. For older friends he made up toasts that <u>lampooned</u> their favorite weakness without causing any offense. The older the friend, the <u>franker</u> the toast.

Student Essay

You may recall the essay by Agnes Kossut in chapter 2 about the day she left her family in Poland to study in the United States. Although today she is far from her father, she feels she can still turn to him in times of trouble.

FATHER

AGNES KOSSUT

"Father, Father, they call me 'Gypsy' because I have long dark   1
hair." The poor voice of a little girl echoed in the house. "Don't worry,
my little daughter. Be wiser than those children and ignore them. You
know how small youngsters call each other names when they quar-
rel."

Those were my father's words of advice. He has always been able to   2
console me when I have had troubles. There were the problems of a
small child and then later those of a young woman. Despite his job,
which occupies much of his time, my father has always been there for
us. He has always put his family first.

My father has always worked to realize his aspirations. When he was   3
a teenager, he began to be interested in sailing. He worked in a yacht

club. When he was 20 years old, he began to build his own yacht. When it was finished, he chartered an extended sailing trip. Through the years, he became a sea captain. In 1978, he set sail on a cruise, alone, from Las Palmas in the Canary Islands through the Bahamas to Miami, Florida. He was the fastest sailor at this distance in all of Poland. He won a prestigious prize for his seamanship.

My father stopped serious sailing because his family was more im- 4 portant to him. However, during vacations, he took our family on the yacht, sailing along the European coast.

There is another thing that impresses me about my father. He is very 5 conscientious about his job. My father is a scientist. He teaches biology and ecology in a university in Poland. In 1980 he began a research project on the life-style of the penguin. He also studied different kinds of mosses. When the Polish government organized a research trip to Antarctica, my father was one of the scientists chosen. For a year and a half he worked in Antarctica, collecting moss and observing penguins in their natural habitat. He wrote many articles, which appeared in scientific journals.

After a number of years, my father had another chance to go to 6 Antarctica to continue his research. However, he declined. His love for his family was more important. I remember him writing a letter to inform the government of his decision: "There is nothing so important to me as my wife and children. I don't want them to be alone. I don't want my children to be raised without their parent." He remained home.

Now I'm almost 18 years old. Living here in the United States, I no 7 longer stand out from my light-haired friends. I haven't heard the nickname "Gypsy" in years. Though my father is on the other side of a great ocean, I know that I can still turn to him.

. . . .

RESPONSE AND ANALYSIS

1. Like Agnes, do you have someone special in your life to whom you turn when you feel vulnerable?

2. Which technique has Agnes used in her introduction?

3. Which aspects about her father has Agnes chosen to develop in her essay?

4. Identify the topic sentences in paragraphs 3 and 5. What specific details does Agnes include to support the topic sentences?

5. How does Agnes connect the conclusion to her essay with the introduction?

Focus on Writing: The Conclusion

Agnes and Addys have each managed to come up with an interesting and appropriate way to end their essays. As with the introductory paragraph, it is not unusual to hear students comment about the difficulty of writing an appropriate conclusion. Let's explore some techniques to consider when you finish the body of your essay and are trying to find an elegant way to indicate that it is coming to an end. You can do many things to conclude your essay; one thing you probably do not want to do, however, is introduce new material. After all, if it is important enough to include in the essay, you should probably not leave it for the conclusion.

. . . .

HIGHLIGHT THE THESIS OR MAIN THEME(S)

Perhaps the most obvious way to approach the conclusion is to highlight the thesis or the main theme(s) developed in your essay. In the conclusion to her essay, "The Right Decision?" in chapter 6, Cui Fang Zhou notes, "Obviously, coming to America has let me gain a lot, despite the losses." This is the thesis she has developed in some detail throughout the essay. Similarly, the last line of Genoveva Díaz's narrative *"Te Quiero, Abuela"* (initially titled, "My First Day in the United States") in chapter 3 reads, "As I was falling asleep, I whispered, *'Te quiero, abuela.'* (I love you, Grandma.)" Although ostensibly writing about her first day in the United States, throughout her essay Genoveva focused on how much she missed her grandmother. In fact, the last line of the essay captured the theme of her essay so well that Genoveva later decided to use it as the title.

. . . .

RETURN TO THE INTRODUCTION

Many writers, as they conclude, return to the introduction (or some other earlier paragraph of the essay) by repeating a key word, phrase, or idea. In the conclusion to her essay about her father in this chapter, Agnes Kossut writes, "I haven't heard the nickname 'Gypsy' in years." This ties in nicely with the introductory paragraph where she writes, "Father, Father, they call me 'Gypsy' because I have long dark hair." Concluding an essay this way gives your writing a neat sense of closure that may be compared to a circle. Imagine a point on a circle (the introduction); follow the outline of the circle (the body of the essay), and return to the point where you began (the conclusion).

....

RELATE THE PERSONAL TO THE UNIVERSAL

When you write about personal themes or provide anecdotal evidence to support your ideas, you may want to conclude with a statement about the wider application of your experiences to give your essay a more universal appeal. Take for example Joel Hernández's essay in chapter 4 about a problem he had because of his limited English, "A Painful Memory." In the conclusion, Joel notes, "I will never forget that day when the teacher screamed at me in public." He then relates his personal experience to others in his situation when he adds, "I wish I could say that was the only problem I encountered due to my limited English, but like so many other immigrants, I could probably write a book." Addys Reynoso does something similar in the conclusion to her essay in this chapter, "Jochy," when she writes, "People say that a dog is a man's best friend. A dog was this young girl's best friend, too."

....

STATE A DECISION OR A BELIEF YOU HAVE REACHED

The word *conclusion* means not only "an ending" but also "a decision or belief reached after the consideration of evidence." You may want to bring your writing to a close by stating a conclusion you have reached based on the theme explored in your essay. See, for example, Andy Sas's essay in chapter 4, "Anxious with English." After relating his unfortunate misunderstanding with his mechanic, Andy concludes that "In order to live in the United States I should start to study English immediately, intensively, and seriously. So I have!"

If you are having trouble writing the conclusion, the problem may actually be with the contents of the body of your essay. Knowing what you want to say in your essay should help you come up with an appropriate way to end it.

1. Go back to the other student essays you have read. Focus on the conclusion. Which of the four techniques (highlight, return, relate, state) has been used? Has any writer used a technique other than those noted earlier? Explain.

2. For further practice, go back to the essays you have written. Revise any conclusion that you feel could be made more effective.

Essay Writing

....

GENERATING IDEAS

In the past you have no doubt been asked to write a *summary* of something you have read in school. To write a good summary, you have to think carefully about what the writer is trying to say. Although some supporting evidence may be included, a good summary will focus on the main ideas of the piece.

Some writers find it helpful to write a summary of the main ideas they intend to develop before writing their first draft. Many novels hundreds of pages in length have been written this way: the author first writes a brief sketch of the characters and the plot development of each chapter. Only when these are completed is the first draft of the story written.

To help you generate ideas in which you describe a friend or family member with whom you have (or have had) a significant relationship, try to write a summary before you write your essay. In your summary, include one or two aspects about the person you intend to focus on as well as number of the supporting details you intend to include.

....

ASSIGNMENT

Use the summary you wrote in the previous activity as the basis for an essay about a friend or a family member with whom you have (or have had) a significant relationship. As you write your essay, you will probably want to add specific details about the person and your relationship that were not included in the summary. When you reach the conclusion, keep in mind the techniques that Addys and Agnes used in the conclusions to their successful pieces, as well as the other techniques discussed in the chapter. After you have written an early draft of your essay, share it with a teacher or a friend and explore possible revisions that would make it even more successful.

9

AT
SCHOOL

. . . .

By the time you have finished high school and gone on to college, you will have come into contact with dozens of professionals who have been responsible for your education and development. Besides your teachers, there are the principals and assistant principals, guidance counselors and other support personnel, coaches, and club advisors. Is there someone you have met at school who stands out?

READING FROM

Famous All Over Town

DANNY SANTIAGO

. . . .

ESTABLISHING THE CONTEXT

Taken collectively, Hispanics comprise the largest ethnic group in the United States outside Americans of European or African descent. Mexican Americans, or Chicanos, are by far the largest of the Hispanic groups. The Mexican American experience began when the United States annexed over one-third of the territory of Mexico in the middle of the nineteenth century. Thousands of Mexican citizens of Texas, Arizona, New Mexico, and California found themselves living under a different and often unsympathetic government.

Because Mexico shares a common border with the United States, immigration to the United States is particularly attractive. In recent decades hundred of thousands of Mexicans have crossed the border—both legally and illegally—in search of a better life. Yet the immigrant experience does not end with those who come here; it continues to the children, grandchildren, and even beyond. For the second generation, the tension between assimilation and maintenance of traditional language and culture is a major concern.

Famous All Over Town, by Danny Santiago, tells the story of Rudy Medina, a young Mexican American growing up among the gangs of Los Angeles. As this excerpt begins, Rudy is in his English class when he is called to meet with his guidance counselor.

. . . .

TO BEGIN

Read the first lines of the selection up to " . . . friends flashed me sympathetic faces and enemies slit their throats with fingernails."

From this first section, what can you learn about the atmosphere in the school and the attitude of Rudy and his classmates toward being there? Bring specific evidence from the text to support your answer.

You will probably come across some unfamiliar words in this excerpt from *Famous All Over Town*. In addition, some common words you may be familiar with are used in a different way. Remember, however, that you can enjoy what you read without knowing the definition or usage of every word. Try to use the context to guess at the unfamiliar words and phrases as you read for your interest and pleasure about Rudy's meeting with his guidance counselor. Don't be overly concerned with words and phrases you don't understand; there will be a vocabulary activity to do after you read, respond to, and analyze the selection.

FROM

FAMOUS ALL OVER TOWN

DANNY SANTIAGO

"Underline every noun," my workbook instructed me. Nouns are said to   1
be the names of persons and things.

"(1) Oscar," I underlined him, "at sixteen was already the best foot-   2
ball player in his school." My workbook was quite sports-minded. Next,
I underlined "sixteen" which was the name of how old this Oscar was.
Or could it be a when-where-how word? I casually glanced around at
my neighbors. Nobody's paper was in view. I erased my underline.

A messenger came in and handed a green slip to Mr. Millstone who   3
was our home-room teacher. I inspected her. She wasn't much to look
at but not as boring as <u>Oscar</u> the sixteen-year-old football hero, or was it
<u>sixteen</u>?

"Medina, Rudy!"   4

I jumped.   5

"Counselor's office."   6

"Oh-oh," somebody said.   7

Counselor is not as dangerous as Vice-principal but bad enough, and   8
when I went up front for my pass, friends flashed me sympathetic faces
and enemies slit their throats with fingernails.

The schoolyard empty looked twice life-size. It was solid blacktop, not   9
clean healthy blacktop but blotchy gray from all our dirty feet. There were
lines painted for basketball and numbers 1 to 12 to line up behind and
wait. Today the sky looked blacktopped too and where it met the yard
you saw chainlink fence. All we lacked was machine-gun towers.

I took a long look round for Sierra, then started off for the Administra-   10 tion building. I felt like an ant walking across that monster yard all by myself and when I tripped on a crack expected the whole world to bust out laughing at me. Where the steps went down, somebody had pulled the handrail loose. I gave it a healthy shake to do my bit, then went wading through plastic cups and dirty napkins by the picnic tables. A squashed Baby Ruth wrapped its loving arms around my shoe. I peeled it off.

"Tssss! Chato!" somebody hollered in a whisper. It was Boxer coming from the Girls'. "Gym's next period and they search us. Act real lovey-dovey, huh? They're watching."   11

I snuggled over to her. She stroked my hair like going steady. And with her other hand slipped me the zip gun. "Get it to Gorilla," she said and left me running. And no time to tell her I was going to the counselor. And no chance to run her down because here's a yard teacher.   12

"Show your pass," he tells me.   13

I did. He followed me into Administration and down the long hall, with Boxer's pistol burning up my pocket. The barrel was a curtain rod with a rubber band-type trigger. It saw a lot of duty among the Veteranos, and once went off in Fat Manuel's pocket. And here I was carrying it into the lion's den. I said a prayer and knocked, what else?   14

"Come in, come in," somebody sang.   15

The previous counselor was your typical wrestler type, but this one was a fat bouncy little man with blue sparkles in his eyes and wild white hair fuzzing out around his head. He didn't look too dangerous, but then you never know.   16

"Rudy Medina? Pilger's the name, Max Pilger. Sit down, son. One million years and you'll never guess why I called you in. The principal just received a letter about you."   17

Now what? People usually complained by phone.   18

"Dear Sir," Mr. Pilger read. "One of your eighth-graders, Rudy Medina, was recently under our care at County Hospital." Oh-oh, their missing thermometer, I thought, but it was Dr. Penrose and he praised me till I didn't know where to look, but suggested special counseling. "So, Mr. Rudy Medina that wants to tack an M.D. on his name, sit back and relax while we talk it over." Relax? With The Goods in my pants pocket? But this new counselor didn't look to be the suspicious type, and he even beamed a smile across his desk at me.   19

"You realize, son, it won't be easy. You need to be tops in every subject, the sciences especially, biology, chemistry, physics. How do you   20 spell gastrointestinal hemorrhoids? You've got to spell them before breakfast. In your sleep you've got to spell them. But God love you, Rudy, thousands of bright boys in your shoes make doctor, so why not you? Let's take a look at your track record."

He opened my folder. Every year they keep a record on you and it 21 follows you like a wolf from school to school.

"Ai-yi-yí," Mr. Pilger said when he saw page one. "C-minus average 22 with a D in Spanish? In *Spanish,* Rudy Medina?"

I didn't mention it but Miss Helstrom's Spanish was from Spain. If 23 you talked Mexican, forget it. Only Anglos got A's with her. Mr. Pilger sighed over every page till he got back to Mrs. Cully and 6th grade at Hibernia. My A's there cheered him up but what surprised him was a certain test they gave that year and IQ was its name.

"135!" he exploded. "Why, son, you scored right off the board." 24

"Just lucky," I apologized. 25

He said there were no luckies on that IQ test, then fired me ques- 26 tions. Did I get sick next term? Did anybody die? Or lose their job? Or how could my score drop forty points in one short year?

"Well," I more or less explained, "my seventh-grade teacher claimed 27 Mrs. Cully cheated on my score."

"A teacher told you that?" Mr. Pilger picked up his pen to make a 28 fiery note of it. "What was her name?"

"Miss Kaplan." 29

"Kaplan?" It seemed to take the heart out of him. "God love you, 30 son," he finally said, "teachers have their bad days like all the rest of us."

The bell sounded off for 5th period. Classroom doors banged open, 31 guys hollered at each other, girls screamed and laughed and happy feet went stampeding down the hall. I wished I could be out there with them, but with that time bomb in my pocket maybe I was better off with this Mr. Pilger. I felt almost safe.

"Rudy," he said when the noise outside quieted down, "in Junior 32 High a lot of bright boys and girls get lost and it's Max Pilger's job to find those buried jewels and bring them to the light."

Could he be meaning me? 33

"Tell me, Rudy," he asked. "How do you honestly feel about 34 Audubon?"

"It's okay, I guess." Who was I to tell him? 35

"Doesn't it bother you that your class is reading at fourth-grade level? 36

Doesn't it bother you that every youngster with a Mexican name gets shunted into Metal Shop or Carpentry?"

"Not the girls," I pointed out. "They take Home Economics."   37

Mr. Pilger sadly shook his head at me. "Hurray for them," he said.   38
"Now tell me frankly, are you learning anything? Do you enjoy *any* of
your classes?"

"Maybe sometimes," I admitted.   39

"Rudy, Rudy, what am I going to do about a boy that one year cracks   40
genius level and next year drops to dull normal?" I looked out the window. Questions like that bother me. "Son, to get two words from you I
need a can opener, and it just happens I have one in stock."

He rustled in his desk and came up with a flat green box. It had   41
the ugly word "test" written on it. No doubt he saw my disgusted
look.

"It won't be graded," he quickly said. "This is strictly between you   42
and me, and nothing to write down." He handed me the craziest picture
I ever saw. It looked like some kindergartener spilled a bunch of paint,
then folded the paper over.

"Huh?" I asked.   43

"'Huh' is right. Now look close and tell me what it's a picture of."   44

"A giant man-eating butterfly," I said. "It's got wings fifty feet across 45
and look, here's blood dripping from its mouth. Bullets couldn't kill it,
so it goes flying around the world eating everyone in sight."

I was pleased with my answer but Mr. Pilger seemed upset. He said   46
there were no rights and wrongs on this particular test but happy danc-
ing girls was what most people seemed to see in that picture. Personally
I don't know how they could unless they were either blind or sex-
minded. So Mr. Pilger put away that test and handed me another. It had
pictures too but more like photographs, and I was to make up a little
story to fit them.

"Easy! They broke the poor guy's guitar," I said.   47

"Where is it broken?"   48

You couldn't exactly see the place but there was this sad-face kid   49
staring at it, so what else?

"Couldn't the boy be daydreaming?" Mr. Pilger asked. "Maybe about   50
the concert he'll some day give at Carnegie Hall?"

"Where's that?" I asked.   51

"And isn't that a violin in his hands?"   52

To my surprise it was. Mr. Pilger handed me more pictures, and I   53 made up stories for him. They were good stories too, with lots of action, but Mr. Pilger wondered why no happy endings?

"That's a sad bunch of pictures," I told him, "so why lie about it?" 54

"The sadness is in you, son," he told me. "I don't see them sad at all." 55

"You're not a Mexican." It popped out of me just-like-that. 56

"Well," he said. "At last. The sleeping giant talks." 57

He looked at me a while. 58

"No, Rudy. I'm not a Mexican. I'm a Jew. Do you know what that means, son? You think you have it tough? We've been discriminated against for two thousand years. You should see the street Max Pilger grew up on. Tenements, son, five stories high and we lived on the top floor. Did the roof leak? It did. Did the landlord fix it? He did not. Toilet? Oh yes, run through the garbage two flights down." 59

Mr. Pilger bounced to his feet, his wild white hair all flying. 60

"Son, you think Audubon is bad? P.S. 153, New York City, was worse. Our teachers hated us. They made fun of our Jewboy haircuts and our oiyoi accents, but we fought those teachers, Rudy. We fought them for good grades. By being two times twice as smart as other kids. We won our A's in spite of them. We made it, Rudy. Through high school, through college and beyond. From my own building came two medical doctors, one now a famous specialist with a very fine practice. Lawyers? By the dozen. Two judges, one of them respected. Yes sir, Mr. Rudy Medina, we made it and I'm going to see you make it too." 61

Mr. Pilger sat down and caught his breath. "Are you willing to cooperate?" 62

I think he really meant it. I think he took an interest. Maybe I had a friend on the other side at last. 63

"I'll try," I told him. 64

"Tomorrow is your new leaf. Come early. Seven A.M. I'll have a ninth-grader there to tutor you. We'll work on English first, and God love you, Rudy, we'll lift that C-minus to an A before the term is over." 65

I believed in him, almost. 66

"Write me out a pass," I reminded. 67

Mr. Pilger clapped his hand on his forehead. "Passes! Fences! Policemen in the restrooms!" he exploded. "What are we running here, a penitentiary?" 68

"More or less, maybe," I told him, and left his office, with my pass in hand and Boxer's zip gun in pocket. 69

· · · · · · · · · · · · · · · · ·

RESPONSE AND ANALYSIS

1. Write for a few minutes in response to what you have read. Besides summarizing, you may want to explore your feelings and thoughts about the reading. It may be helpful to consider these categories:

   a. what you understood about the reading

   b. something that puzzled you in the reading

   c. something you would like to discuss with the writer or one of the characters

   d. a memory the reading evoked

   e. how you felt about the reading

2. Several characters are mentioned in the reading. Use the context of the story to identify each:

   a. Mr. Millstone

   b. Chato

   c. Boxer

   d. Gorilla

   e. the Veteranos

   f. Fat Manuel

   g. Max Pilger

   h. Dr. Penrose

   i. Miss Helstrom

   j. Mrs. Cully

   k. Miss Kaplan

3. A recurring theme in *Famous All Over Town* is the involvement of Rudy and his friends in gangs. Where in the reading does this appear? Make specific reference to the text.

4. What sort of man is Max Pilger? Bring specific evidence from the text to support your description. How does he compare with the guidance counselors you have had?

5. To understand Rudy better so that he may help him, Pilger administers a psychological diagnostic, the *Rorschach test*. In this test, subjects describe what they see in a series of inkblots, thereby revealing aspects of their personality through their responses. What does Mr. Pilger learn from Rudy's interpretations of the inkblots? Using an encyclopedia or other reference material, prepare a short report on the Rorschach test.

6. Mr. Pilger speaks at some length about being Jewish. Why does he mention this? How is this relevant to Rudy's situation?

. . . .

FURTHER EXPLORATION OF LANGUAGE AND LITERATURE:
THE NARRATOR

To tell their stories, writers use two kinds of narrators in works of fiction: the *first-person narrator* and the *omniscient narrator*. The first person narrator is a character in the story. *Famous All Over Town* is narrated by Rudy, the main character in the novel. Another example of the first-person narrator is found in the excerpt from *How the García Girls Lost Their Accents* (chapter 3), narrated by Yolanda.

The word omniscient comes from two Latin words meaning "all knowing." The omniscient narrator knows everything that is essential for the successful telling of the story. The narrator may jump from past to present describing the feelings and thoughts of all the characters as well as the setting and plot of the story. The excerpt from *In the Year of the Boar and Jackie Robinson* (chapter 5) is told through this type of narration.

It is tempting to confuse the author with the narrator, but remember—there is a difference. The writer is a person of flesh and blood. A narrator, whether first person or omniscient, is a creation of the writer and exists in the work of fiction only.

Go back to the literature you have read so far in this book. For each selection, decide which type of narration is used: first-person or omniscient. Bring specific evidence from the text to support your answer.

. . . .

VOCABULARY: FIGURATIVE LANGUAGE

As Rudy walks to meet with his counselor, he notes that the zip gun he was carrying was "burning" in his pocket. You are probably familiar with the *literal* or most common definition of the word burn, "to be on fire." Here, however, Rudy is using the word in a *figurative* or an unusual and imaginative way to suggest that he was so conscious of the pistol in his pocket, it felt *as if* it were burning there.

You probably have come across a familiar word that did not seem to make sense in its context. One possibility is that while you were familiar with the literal definition of the word, you may have had trouble completely understanding its figurative usage. For example, when Mr. Pilger learns that one of Rudy's former teachers has suggested that Rudy's high IQ score was obtained by cheating, he "picked up his pen to make a fiery note of it." Consider that emotion and passion are commonly compared to fire. What sort of note, then, would a fiery note be?

A. Explain the figurative language in the following sentences from *Famous All Over Town*. To clearly explain the figurative usage, it might be helpful to refer to the literal definition as well.

Example

I felt like an ant walking across that monster yard all by myself.

In its literal sense a *monster* is a horrible creature, often quite large. Here Rudy uses the phrase *monster yard* to convey figuratively how large and unfriendly that area of school looked to him.

1. "135!" he exploded. "Why, son, you scored right off the board."

2. It seemed to take the heart out of him.

3. " . . . in Junior High a lot of bright boys and girls get lost and it's Max Pilger's job to find those buried jewels and bring them to the light."

4. "Son, to get two words from you I need a can opener, and it just happens I have one in stock."

5. Tomorrow is your new leaf.

B. Identify and explain other examples of figurative language in the reading.

Student Essay

Do you recall the difficult encounter that Andrzej Sas from Poland had with his mechanic when Andy first came to the United States ("Anxious with English," chapter 4)? In this essay, he describes a wonderful teacher he had years before in his homeland.

A MEMORABLE TEACHER
ANDRZEJ SAS

I once heard it said that good teachers are born, not made. If so, my science teacher from high school in Poland was born to teach.

I had chosen a high school with a special program in biology and chemistry and I had four to six hours of those subjects each week. Mrs. Slawinska was my biology teacher for four years. She always explained everything in an easy way and was always patient and helpful. "Don't be afraid to ask if you don't understand something," she always reminded us. "We don't have stupid questions, we only have stupid answers."

For four years she revealed the secrets of nature to us through experiments, lectures, and field trips to museums, universities, and hospitals. I will never forget the visit to a hospital where we saw an autopsy being performed. Everybody was shocked and our classmate Anna even fainted. After that I was sure that I could not become a doctor!

In Poland we don't pay for education in the university; however, we   4
have to pass some very difficult tests in order to be admitted. Some fields are very popular, so getting into the university to study those majors is particularly competitive. Because so many students want to study medicine, only those with the best academic record are accepted to study biology. Mrs. Slawinska organized a group of students who were especially interested in that subject. She prepared us for the Polish Academic Olympics in biology, which takes place every year. The first- and third-place winners came from our group. As a reward, they were accepted into the university to study biology without having to pass those very difficult entrance exams. Not only was it a great moment for the students, but for Professor Slawinska as well.

She treated us like her own children. We could talk to her about per-   5
sonal problems. Mrs. Slawinska always gave us good advice and helped us. I remember one incident that happened in our third grade, as we call the junior year of high school in Poland. Barbara was one of the students in our class. Her mother had died when she was 15 and her father was an alcoholic. Barbara wanted to finish high school but her father was against it. Mrs. Slawinska arranged for her to get special counseling and financial aid. She organized extra tutoring and the best three or four students from our class would meet with Barbara every week to help her study and do the homework. I can still recall our graduation day, with Barbara proudly holding her diploma.

After we finished our junior year, Mrs. Slawinska asked us to call her   6
by her first name, Bozena. This was very unusual, because the relationship between students and teachers in Poland is usually very formal and distant. As a result, Mrs. Slawinska, Bozena, gained even more respect and affection.

I finished high school almost 15 years ago and I still have contact   7
with Mrs. Slawinska. I always send her holiday greetings on her name day, a special day for Poles. She will always be in my memory.

. . . .

RESPONSE AND ANALYSIS

1. Andrzej starts his essay with the general observation that "good teachers are born, not made." What does this statement mean to you? Have you ever had a teacher you felt was born to teach?

2. Andrzej concentrates on two main themes in his description of Mrs. Slawinska: her ability to teach the subject and the personal relationship she had with her students. List the supporting evidence he provides for each theme.

3. Mrs. Slawinska's physical appearance is not mentioned. Does this detract from the description of the teacher? Explain.

4. A number of times in the essay Andrzej provides an explanation of the education system in Poland. For example, in paragraph 4 he mentions the difficult college entrance exams. Where else does Andrzej provide an explanation for an audience who might know little of schooling in Poland?

Focus on Writing: Journal Writing Revisited

If you have been writing in your journal consistently, by this point you have probably written a great deal. Have you come to look forward to this activity? Has it helped you to become a better writer?

One student who found keeping a journal especially important is Lei Zhang, whose essay about cultural contrasts between the United States and China appears in chapter 5. In the following essay about a memorable educator, Lei wrote about Mr. Lee, his twelfth-grade Chinese teacher. Like Andy, in order to describe his teacher, Lei focuses on the personality of the man and his dedication as well as on one of his favorite teaching techniques: Mr. Lee had his students keep a journal.

A TEACHER WHO HELPED ME SUCCEED

LEI ZHANG

Mr. Lee was my 12th-grade Chinese teacher. At that time, like all Chinese high school students, I was facing the competitive college entrance test. On one part of the test we were required to write an essay on a topic of which we had no prior knowledge. I felt very anxious about this part because I had little confidence in my ability to write Chinese.   1

In order to improve our writing in a relatively short period of time, Mr. Lee asked us to keep a journal every day. At first, this was difficult for me. I tried to write my observations about life. Although I did not write particularly well in my journal, Mr. Lee would make detailed suggestions on how to improve.   2

In class, he always showed examples of effective journal entries from the students. These would be analyzed. This helped me a lot and after   3 several weeks, I found that it was not so very hard to keep a journal. Sometimes I wrote what I thought about the news. Sometimes I wrote about what was going on in my life at the time. After I finished reading an essay for one of my classes in school, I would write what I felt about it in my journal. I began to feel that writing was no longer an unpleasant task. Because I kept writing in my journal, my writing quickly improved.

Mr. Lee was very concerned about his students. As the entrance 4
exam approached, I studied so hard that I became sick. I had to miss several classes. When Mr. Lee learned of this, he came to my house and gave me my lessons at home. This made a deep impression on me. When the day of the test arrived, I felt confident that I could do the essay part. When the results were made known and I learned that I had passed and was accepted into college, I knew that I had Mr. Lee to thank.

I could not have succeeded without Mr. Lee. He was a great teacher. 5

. . . .

ANALYSIS

Lei mentions the kinds of topics he would write about in his journal: his observations about life, his thoughts about the news, matters related to his personal life, and responses to his schoolwork. The comments his teacher would make helped Lei to improve his writing. But perhaps even more important, keeping a journal every day helped Lei feel more comfortable with writing. Writing became something to look forward to. How do your own experiences with journal writing compare with Lei's?

You might like to evaluate your journal writing experiences by writing a journal entry *about* journal writing. Start by rereading your journal. Then write for few minutes in response to what you have read. Explore your feelings and thoughts about your journal and about the activity of journal writing. Use the questions below as a guide, but feel free to consider anything related to the topic.

Which entries give you the most pleasure?

Which themes recur more than once in your journal? How is this significant?

Has keeping a journal helped you with your more formal essay writing? Why do you think this is so or not so?

Which entries might you like to expand into a formal essay?

If you feel comfortable doing so, after you have written your journal entry share it with your classmates. Then for your next journal entry, explore how their journal writing experiences compare with your own.

Essay Writing

GENERATING IDEAS

Freewrite about a teacher or someone else involved in your schooling. You may want to use the categories below as a guide, but feel free to consider anything related to the topic.

a. background information

b. physical description

c. professional aspects and supporting material

d. personality and supporting material

e. a memorable quotation

f. how you have been influenced

. . . .

ASSIGNMENT

Use your freewriting as the basis for an essay in which you describe a teacher, guidance counselor, coach, or any member of the school staff about whom you have strong associations, either positive or negative. Keep in mind how Andrzej and Lei approached this topic in their successful essays. They developed two main themes— the personality and abilities of their subjects—providing specific supporting evidence and necessary background information. After you have written an early draft of your essay, share it with a teacher or a friend and explore possible revisions that would make it even more successful.

10

PLACES

· · · · · · · · · · · · · · · ·

Most people have an emotional bond to some place where they feel a particular sense of belonging. For many of those who have left the land of their birth, that place is miles and memories away. Some have been able to capture that feeling where they have relocated. Have you?

Sweet Promised Land

ROBERT LAXALT

· · · · · · · · · · · · · · · ·

ESTABLISHING THE CONTEXT

Like many minorities throughout the world, the Basque are a people with a distinct ethnic identity but without their own independent country. The Basque homeland lies in the mountainous region on the border between France and Spain. Although Basque immigration never reached the levels of the other peoples mentioned so far, thousands of Basque did settle in the western United States, where many worked as sheep herders. More recently, with the spread of legalized gambling in the United States, small communities of Basque have been established in Connecticut and Florida. Betting on *jai alai,* a Basque game, is a popular attraction in those cities, and most of the best players are recruited from the Basque homeland in Europe.

In *Sweet Promised Land,* Robert Laxalt writes about the life of his father, Dominique, a Basque immigrant who settled in Nevada, where he worked and prospered as a sheep herder. One critic wrote that the book "speaks not only for the Basques, but for the Italians and the Yugoslavs, for the Swedes and the Irish, the Portuguese and the Greeks—all our second generation citizens." In this excerpt, Dominique, accompanied by his son and his sister, has returned to the place of his birth for the first time since coming to the United States almost fifty years earlier.

· · · · · · · · · · · · · · · ·

TO BEGIN

1. Have you returned to your homeland for a visit since coming to the United States? Describe the visit. If not, try to imagine how it would be to return after an extended absence.

2. Read the first two paragraphs of the selection. Notice the many details that pro-

vide a physical description of the area where the father's birthplace is located, appealing to the sense of sight with references to color. List these.

3. As you continue reading, pay particular attention to the many other descriptive passages. Afterward you will be asked to make a list of phrases that provide a physical description of the father's birthplace.

You will probably come across some unfamiliar words in this excerpt from *Sweet Promised Land*. Remember, however, that you can enjoy and understand what you read without knowing the definition of every word. Try to use the context to guess at the unfamiliar words and phrases as you read for your interest and pleasure about Dominique Laxalt's return to his birthplace. Don't be overly concerned with words and phrases you don't understand; there will be a vocabulary activity to do after you read, respond to, and analyze the selection.

FROM

SWEET PROMISED LAND

ROBERT LAXALT

It was autumn afternoon, and the air was rich with the scents of ripened   1
fields. In the times of silence, there was the drone of insects hurrying to
finish their business before end of day. The fern-covered slopes that
stretched toward the high Pyrenees were red with color, and in the distance the tall poplars that marked my father's home were tipped with
gold.

Once, when the road passed a place of high ground and the property   2
lay before us in full view, my father stopped and tipped back his hat and
stood a long moment looking at it. Beyond the stand of poplars, the
house loomed with its curving black roof and stone walls that tapered to
one end and gave way to the low, sod-covered barn. And beyond that
rose green fields where, even now, we could see the handful of sleek
brown work cows and shining white sheep grazing together beneath the
apple and walnut trees.

Until that moment, my father had been cheerful and talkative on the   3
walk from Tardets. But now, he fell quiet. His head was bent as if he
were afraid to look at too much of what was around him, and his steps
as we descended from the rise were almost reluctant. His sister, Marie-
Jeanne, who had come with us, said nothing but only looked at me with
a little closing of her eyes.

Where the road turned off into the dirt path that rose to the property, 4
there was a low, stone fence with moss growing soft over the top and in
the cracks, and when we paused there my father leaned with his back
against the fence to look at the pasture, and when he did his fingers unconsciously found their way to the cracks and gently rubbed the moss
that was there.

An old work cow with long and graceful horns, who had been stand- 5
ing beneath a walnut tree, looked up at our approach and then came
slowly down to the fence where my father stood. He took her head in
his hands and pulled it back and forth and reached over and smoothed
the worn place where the yoke had made its mark, and murmured to
her, "*Gaichoa.* If I didn't know better, I would think you were my own
old friend."

He took her by the horns and pushed her head back into the pasture, 6
and said to us, "I wonder if we should go to the house after all. I hate to
bother the people when they're probably so busy."

"They are expecting us," said Marie-Jeanne. "I sent word that we 7
were coming to visit, so I think that we had better go in."

My father shrugged and led the way up the winding path. The way 8
turned for the last time and we could see through the iron grating of the
high gate the house suddenly and intimately before us. But when he put
his hands on the gate and began to open it, there was a rusty, creaking
sound, and he stopped again, as if listening.

There was a flagstone walk with grass growing through the rocks that 9
led to the front door, and on both sides of the walk there were berry
bushes and old, gnarled trees. When we reached the doorstep, Marie-
Jeanne went up to knock, but before she could the door opened to
frame a young Basque woman and, peering from behind her long skirts,
a little girl.

"*Aintzina,*" the woman said with a smile. 10

The room was big and shadowy, with walls and floor of stone, and at 11
the far end a fireplace with a cooking pot hanging in it, and above a
mantel with brass and copper utensils glinting in the dim light. There
was a long wooden table in the middle of the floor, and the young husband of the house was standing beside it, smiling bashfully.

We sat down on the wooden benches while the young wife brought 12
wine and glasses to the table. She looked strangely at my father when
he sat down without looking around once, but instead began to talk to
the young man. She said nothing until we had finished our wine, and
then she said to him, "Can you remember where you slept?"

He nodded and gestured with his head to a room at the side, and   13
then turned away to talk to the husband again. In a little while, she
spoke about it again. "Don't you want to see the room?" And then, not
waiting for his answer, she took him by the hand. "Come see it."

He went with her then, and through the doorway we could see him   14
looking about. But the only thing he said was, "I remember that crack in
the wall, the one almost like a face."

When he came back into the big room, Marie-Jeanne was standing at   15
an old, high-backed wooden bench beside the fireplace. There was a
sewing basket on the seat.

"Do you remember this, Dominique?" she asked. "Do you remember   16
Mamma sewing here by the firelight?"

I think he turned before he realized what she was going to say, be-   17
cause his eyes narrowed with pain and a little sound was torn out of
him. Then, the mask fell again over his face, and he went to the table
and picked up his hat and began to thank the young couple for their
hospitality and to tell them that we had to be going. Despite their
protests, he said good-by and went to the door to wait for us.

The first twilight came as we were returning to Tardets, and the val-   18
ley was wrapped with the warm glow of afterday, touching everything
with a softness that was almost unreal. But down the path and the long
road, never once did my father look back.

· · · · · · · · · · · · · · · · ·

RESPONSE AND ANALYSIS

1. Write for a few minutes in response to what you have read. Besides summarizing,
   you may want to explore your feelings and thoughts about the reading. It may be
   helpful to consider these categories:

   a. what you understood about the reading

   b. something that puzzled you in the reading

   c. something you would like to discuss with the writer or one of the characters

   d. a memory the reading evoked

   e. how you felt about the reading

2. Make a list of the phrases that provide a physical description of the father's birthplace.

3. Twice during the excerpt a phrase in the Basque language is used: *Gaichoa* and
   Aintzina. Using context clues, try to guess what these phrases might mean.

4. When Marie-Jeanne reminds her brother of their mother sewing by the firelight, we are told that "the mask fell again over his face." What does this phrase communicate to you?

5. As Dominique leaves his childhood home, his son notes, "never once did my father look back." Why do you think the father acts this way? In contrast, you may recall that it is said of Nils Vaag, the young Norwegian fisherman in *The Boat of Longing* (chapter 1), "Having got a little way off, he had to look back." Discuss the different reactions of the two characters, Nils and Dominique, upon leaving their homelands.

. . . .

FURTHER EXPLORATION OF LANGUAGE AND LITERATURE: LITERARY REFERENCES

You have already seen how writers refer to historical events or aspects of culture without explaining them. It is assumed that educated readers will understand the references or will be curious enough to want to investigate them by themselves. Another type of reference is a *literary reference,* a reference to a well-known work of literature. Probably the most widely read books in the world are the many books of the Bible. The title *Sweet Promised Land* makes a reference to the biblical story of Abraham.

1. The story of Abraham begins in the book of Genesis, the first book of the Old Testament. Read chapter 12, verses 1–7.

2. After you have read the story of Abraham, explain the connection between the biblical story and the phrase *Sweet Promised Land.* Why do you think Laxalt chose the phrase for the title of the story of his immigrant father?

. . . .

VOCABULARY

In the following passages, try to determine the meaning of each underlined word by its context. (You may want to choose additional words from the reading if you found the vocabulary very challenging.) Then provide a dictionary definition either in English or in your native language. Finally, read the excerpt from *Sweet Promised Land* a second time, paying close attention to the words you have learned as well as the other points discussed in the previous activities.

1. His head was bent as if he were afraid to look at too much of what was around him, and his steps as we descended from the rise were almost <u>reluctant.</u>

2. ...when we <u>paused</u> there my father leaned with his back against the fence to look at the <u>pasture,</u> and when he did his fingers unconsciously found their way to the cracks and gently rubbed the <u>moss</u> that was there.

3. He took her head in his hands and pulled it back and forth and reached over and smoothed the worn place where the <u>yoke</u> had made its mark, and <u>murmured</u> to her, "<u>*Gaichoa.*</u>"

4. But when he put his hands on the gate and began to open it, there was a rusty, <u>creaking</u> sound, and he stopped again, as if listening.

5. There was a long wooden table in the middle of the floor, and the young husband of the house was standing beside it, smiling <u>bashfully.</u>

6. ...he went to the table and picked up his hat and began to thank the young couple for their <u>hospitality</u> and to tell them that we had to be going.

Student Essay

Do your childhood memories include a special place? For Tania Vargas, that place is the bedroom of her home back in the Dominican Republic.

EL PALOMAR

TANIA VARGAS

Passersby could always hear music and laughter coming from the second floor. The white curtains rustled in the windows of the building my father had built and painted blue to recall a tropical sky. It was my bedroom in the Dominican Republic. Papi would affectionately call it *El Palomar,* because it reminded him of a bird house. There were always birds on the zinc roof atop the bedroom of his little dove.

Every Saturday I would invite my friends over. There would always be those confidential conversations between girls about boyfriends and love. We used to put on my older sister's miniskirts and her lace blouses. All dressed up we would dance the merengue pretending to front an orchestra as the radio played the latest hit. When we got tired we would play with my Barbie dolls. No afternoon passed without all of us jumping on the beds throwing pillows at each other. Later we would go downstairs for cake, juice, and fruit.

My bedroom was the perfect spot for me and my friends to spend

Saturday. We didn't think about problems. We felt no responsibilities. School was far from our thoughts. It was Saturday! Why think of school? It was a day for fun; a time to be together to see the smiles appear on our faces.

Sometimes some friends would sleep over and we had a pajama   4
party. I remember when my friend Jenny and I lay in bed and she gave me a small red fruit and told me that it was a cherry. I bit into it and started to scream for water. She had given me a hot pepper to eat. Tears streamed down my cheeks. Was it because it felt like my whole mouth was on fire or because I felt so foolish? Later my friend apologized and told me, "I'm sorry, Tania. I really didn't want to make you cry." I looked at her with an angry face but then I started to laugh and she joined in. We spent the whole night talking and telling silly scary stories. Through the window we could see the moon and the stars.

When it was time for my friends to leave, I was comforted by the   5
thought that they would come over the following week. I turned the radio off but I was already imagining that next Saturday the music and laughter would once again be heard from the window of my bedroom.

. . . .

RESPONSE AND ANALYSIS

1. Explain the title of the essay.

2. Tania includes a number of phrases that provide a physical description of her bedroom. List these.

3. Besides the descriptive phrases, Tania relates a number of anecdotes set in her bedroom involving her and her friends. Briefly summarize these.

4. How old do you think Tania and her friends are at the time of this essay? Bring specific evidence from the essay to support your opinion.

5. Which technique has Tania used to write the conclusion to her essay?

Focus on Writing: Peer Revision

An ancient piece of wisdom goes something like this: Give a man a fish and he eats for one day; teach him how to fish and he never goes hungry. The same idea is true of school: a good education gives students the ability to continue to learn on their own outside of a formal classroom setting. The activities in this textbook have been designed to help you to help yourselves with your education and your study of English by encouraging you to learn on your own. As you continue to determine meaning from context, explore unfamiliar references, analyze and respond to texts, and put your ideas into writing, you will become even better readers and writers of English.

After each essay assignment, you have been encouraged to share your writing with your classmates in order to give and receive feedback, a process called *peer revision*. It is not unusual for students to feel uncomfortable with peer revision initially. Many note their inexperience with analyzing and responding to the writing of others. By now, however, you have already examined a good number of the elements of successful writing. You have seen the importance of revision. You may feel that you are better prepared not only to revise your own work but to help others revise theirs.

Understand that most people are sensitive about sharing their writing with others. So, to make peer revision a meaningful activity and one you will want to continue, keep a few common sense points in mind.

- Start by pointing out something you liked about the essay. There is something positive to say about almost any piece of writing: the interesting choice of topic, the emotion that the writer feels about the material, or any one of the elements reviewed in the following pages. Saying something good about the essay will help to establish a productive working relationship.

- Simply identifying something you didn't understand or something you'd like to know more about can be helpful. An observation, such as "I'm not quite sure what you mean here" or "I'd like to know more about something you've said here," can help the writer make necessary revisions.

- Avoid making negative comments that are overly general. A remark such as "You don't say anything important about bilingual education in your essay" provides no real help. Instead, offer constructive suggestions about specific elements in the essay: "You might want to mention an anecdote here about someone you know who has benefited from bilingual education."

Keep these points in mind not only during peer revision but when you revise your own work. Students are often unnecessarily critical of themselves. Remember that writing is a process, and you should feel gratified by the improvement you show even when you are not completely satisfied with the final product.

Focus on Writing:
Review—Elements of the Essay

At this point, let's review some elements of successful writing that we have explored earlier. Be sure to go back to the essays referred to, which illustrate the specific element under discussion. Notice that each item begins with a question. You can use these questions later as you help your classmates revise their work and as you revise your own.

· · · · · · · · · · · · · · · ·

THE FOCUS

Does the essay focus on one or two specific themes? Could the essay be improved by developing one or two themes in greater detail while omitting others? For example, Pedro Batista saw, heard, thought, felt, and did many things on his first days in the United States ("My First Days in New York," in chapter 3). However, he chose to develop two or three themes in some detail rather than try to include a little bit about everything. Remember the proverb, Don't bite off more than you can chew.

· · · · · · · · · · · · · · · ·

THE TITLE

Does the title of the essay accurately reflect what the essay is about? Sometimes a writer may choose a title that gives the reader a clear idea of the theme of the essay. This is what Agnes Kossut did with "Leaving Home" (chapter 1). Other times the title makes a reference to the text that doesn't become completely clear until you finish reading the essay. The title of Joel Hernández's essay about his experiences learning English, "A Painful Memory" (chapter 4), is not really understood until the essay is completed.

· · · · · · · · · · · · · · · ·

PARAGRAPHS

Have the ideas in the essay been organized into paragraphs? Have the paragraphs been organized around a main idea stated in a topic sentence and accompanied by supporting material? When Cui Fang Zhou revised her essay "The Right Decision?" (chapter 6), she added the topic sentence to paragraph 3: "I have also given up much in my social and family life." This was followed by specific supporting material on how her life has changed in those areas. In addition, in the early draft of her essay, Cui Fang included in the same paragraph the theme of changes in her work life together with the theme of changes in her social and family life; in the final version, she put the different themes in separate paragraphs. Sometimes a little reorganization can convey the ideas of an essay more effectively without making significant changes in the content.

. . . .

THESIS STATEMENT

Is there a thesis statement of the essay's main idea? In the opening paragraph of his essay "When In Rome" (chapter 5), Lei Zhang states his thesis explicitly: "I have noticed a number of differences between the codes of conduct of the two countries [China and the United States]. These differences may create misunderstandings." This idea is developed throughout the essay with specific examples. Sometimes the thesis of the essay may not be stated so directly. For example, in her essay "El Palomar" (this chapter), Tania Vargas never states explicitly that her bedroom was a place of special significance to her. However, the idea is made clear through the description and anecdotes she includes in her essay.

. . . .

THE INTRODUCTION

Is the introduction to the essay effective? You have seen that sometimes the writer will first introduce the theme of the essay in a general way before moving on to the specifics. Andy Sas does this in "A Memorable Teacher" (chapter 9) when he writes in the introduction: "I once heard it said that good teachers are born, not made. If so, my science teacher from high school in Poland was born to teach." Other times, the writer may want to move directly into the topic in order to catch the reader's attention. This is what Genoveva Díaz does in her essay *"Te Quiero, Abuela"* (initially titled, "My First Day in the United States") (chapter 3) when she begins with the direct quotation, "As soon as we arrive in the United States, your Dad and I will take you all to a nice restaurant."

. . . .

SPECIFIC DETAILS

Are there specific details to help convey the writer's ideas? In her essay "Father" (chapter 8), Agnes Kossut writes that her father put his family ahead of his career.

She demonstrates this by telling about his refusal to continue his research on Antarctica, even quoting from a letter he wrote to the Polish government. In her essay "Different Cultures" (chapter 5), Cui Fang Zhou not only states the differences between China and the United States, she shows them by providing specific examples she has observed at the airport and at school.

. . . .

DIRECT QUOTATION/REPORTED SPEECH

Has the writer used direct quotation and reported speech appropriately? Using direct quotation is one of the most effective ways to make your writing sound authentic. In his essay "Riding on a Lonely Train" (chapter 1), Eric Guzmán recalls the parting words of his mother, whom he left behind in Honduras: "Take care of yourself, my son. Study hard and make your mother proud." You will probably want to use direct quotation in cases where the words spoken are particularly meaningful. If not, it is probably preferable to use reported speech. For example, in "Anxious with English" (chapter 4), Andrzej Sas calls his boss when he finds himself in a difficult situation. He simply writes, "I decided to call my boss and ask for help. Fortunately, he was a generous man and he helped me out of my trouble." Andy had decided that the actual words of the conversation were not important enough to include.

. . . .

EXPLANATION OF REFERENCES

Are there references in the essay that may be unfamiliar to the audience? Do these references require further explanation? In "Leaving Home" (chapter 1), when Agnes Kossut mentions the car ride to Warsaw, she adds, "where there is an international airport." Similarly, when Ana Vásquez mentions Fernandito Villalona in "A Special Feeling" (chapter 7), she explains that he is "a famous Dominican musician." Understanding who your audience is can help you decide which references require explanation and which do not.

. . . .

LANGUAGE

Are there any phrases that you especially like? Recall the phrases Zuyapa Guzmán uses to describe the physical sensation she felt on the flight from Mexico in "Destination: The United States/Destiny: Unknown" (chapter 2): "My stomach moved from one way to another like a washing machine. My heart began beating fast like it does when I see a horror movie." Interesting use of language not only helps convey your ideas more clearly, it makes your writing more enjoyable to read.

. . . .

THE CONCLUSION

Does the essay end with an appropriate conclusion? Lei Zhang concludes "A Teacher Who Helped Me Succeed" about his teacher (chapter 9) with a clear statement of his thesis: "I could not have succeeded without Mr. Lee. He was a great teacher." Yessenia Briceño connects the conclusion of her essay "In the Air" (chapter 2) to the introduction through the idea of tears: tears of sadness and tears of joy. Addys Reynoso relates the special relationship she had with her cousin's dog Jochy (chapter 8) to the general sentiment many people have for dogs by quoting a well-known proverb: A dog is a man's best friend. There are many ways to conclude an essay; the key is to do so elegantly.

Essay Writing

. . . .

GENERATING IDEAS

You have seen the importance of generating ideas as an initial step in the process of writing an essay. As one writing teacher once said, "You don't write writing; you write something." To help you decide on the "something" to write about, various techniques have been suggested: thinking about the topic and taking notes, freewriting, brainstorming with others, writing a summary, and reviewing your journal entries. As a next step, many writers find that preparing an outline helps them to develop and organize their ideas as they proceed to write the first draft of their essay.

You will probably find that at certain times one technique will help you generate ideas for your writing, while at other times a different technique will be more helpful. Choose whatever techniques you feel will work best as you generate ideas for an essay in which you describe a place of special significance in your life.

. . . .

ASSIGNMENT

Use the ideas you generated in the previous activity as the basis of an essay in which you describe a place of special significance in your life. Keep in mind how Tania Vargas approached this topic in her successful essay: in addition to providing a description of her bedroom, she related some anecdotes that took place there. After you have written an early draft of your essay, share it with a classmate. Use the section "Review: Elements of the Essay" in this chapter as you engage in peer revision to make your essay even more successful.

AT
WORK

. . . .

The promise of better employment is often the main factor behind the decision to leave one's homeland. What sort of experiences are you familiar with from the world of work in the United States?

READING FROM

New Americans: An Oral History

AL SANTOLI

. . . .

ESTABLISHING THE CONTEXT

At the turn of the century, a great number of Chinese contract laborers arrived to work in the sugar plantations of Hawaii. With them came a few thousand Koreans. However, large-scale immigration from Korea began only several generations later, after the resolution of the Korean War. Since the passing into law of the Immigration and Nationality Act of 1965, more than a half-million Koreans have immigrated to the United States. Korean Americans now comprise one of the largest and fastest-growing Asian American communities in the United States. Although Korean Americans may be found throughout the American labor force, they have become particularly distinguished for their entrepreneurial spirit and successful small businesses.

The reading in this chapter comes from *New Americans: An Oral History* by Al Santoli. What is an oral history? Your introduction to the study of history has probably been through textbooks based on scholarly research. An oral history, however, attempts to show how things were—or are—primarily through interviews. *New Americans* is a collection of *transcripts,* or written records of conversations, with recent immigrants to the United States. In the following excerpt, Cha Ok Kim tells how, while still holding down a job in a clothing factory, he also began to work as a *peddler*—someone who sells small goods on the street or while traveling from place to place—and eventually built a multimillion-dollar business.

. . . .

TO BEGIN

1. In what ways would you expect an oral history to be different from the other readings you have studied?

2. What does the phrase "New Americans" communicate to you?

3. Is there a tradition of peddling in your homeland? Do you see many peddlers where you live in the United States? Discuss some of the advantages and disadvantages of making a living by peddling.

4. You will probably come across some unfamiliar words in this excerpt from *New Americans*. Sometimes it helps to familiarize yourself with key vocabulary before you begin reading. The underlined words are all related to the world of commerce and business. In the following passages, try to determine the meaning of each word by its context. Then provide a dictionary definition either in English or in your native language.

   a. We were able to buy wigs for $3 apiece in <u>bulk</u> orders. On weekends I would go into the streets and sell them.

   b. Then I found out where the black neighborhoods, where people appreciated our low-cost <u>merchandise,</u> were in Boston, Cleveland, and Detroit.

   c. In the mornings I would go from store to store, from 9:00 A.M. until mid-afternoon, collecting wholesale orders from <u>merchants.</u>

   d. When a policeman would check me out, I would show my New York sales license. Sometimes that would be legal. But other times I had to purchase a <u>permit</u> at the local city hall.

   e. All the money we made, we <u>reinvested</u> to keep our business growing.

   f. They said, "You purchase the wigs <u>wholesale,</u> and we will buy from you for ourselves to sell." That's business, right?

   g. I named my company Dong Jin, "Going East," because I <u>imported</u> from Asia.

   h. At first, my wife and I used our apartment as our <u>warehouse</u> and office.

   i. I didn't have the $10,000 necessary to put down on my store, so a friend <u>cosigned</u> for a bank loan.

   j. With a twenty-foot ceiling, we were able to build a <u>loft</u> to use as our business office. And we have five hundred square feet in the basement for storage.

   k. Other Korean friends had the same experience with the banks, so we decided to form our own <u>credit union</u> or investment corporation.

   l. But in New York City, a store owner can lose his business because of <u>skyrocketing</u> [increases]. Some rents in this area have jumped from $1,000 a month to more than $10,000 in just five years.

   m. The products we sell come in large quantity from Korea, Taiwan, China, Japan. Large <u>shipments</u> come into the warehouse every week.

   n. We use different machines in an <u>assembly line</u>: cutting, stamping holes, inserting buckles.

o. During the course of a year, we are doing around $4–5 million worth of <u>trans-actions.</u>

p. We make a five- to six-percent <u>net</u> profit on that amount. We have to pay the <u>overhead</u> on our store, taxes, salaries for our workers, and other expenses.

The language of an oral history is often less challenging than it is in other *genres,* or types, of literature. Nevertheless, there may be other unfamiliar words in this excerpt. Remember, however, that you can still enjoy and understand what you read without knowing the definition of every word. Try to use the context to guess at the unfamiliar words and phrases as you read for your interest and pleasure about Kim's rise from peddler to successful businessman. Don't be overly concerned with words and phrases you don't understand.

FROM

NEW AMERICANS: AN ORAL HISTORY

AL SANTOLI

My wife went to various wholesale stores during the days, while I worked at the factory. We were able to buy wigs for $3 apiece in bulk orders. On weekends I would go into the streets and sell them. I started out peddling in Harlem.   1

I put fifty wigs in a cloth bag that I carried over my shoulder. I would walk into any place—restaurants, bars, hospitals, and door to door. I learned to stand in a visible place on the sidewalk. I'd pull a wig out of the bag and start combing it. Ladies would come up and ask what I was doing. I would pull a few wigs out of the bag to show them the different styles. I'd say, "Do you like red? Okay, here's red." That wasn't so dangerous, because I dealt with ladies only. But sometimes men followed me, looking for a chance to rob me.   2

In one day of selling wigs I could make as much money as one week in the factory. So I left the textile job and expanded my selling trips to Newark and Philadelphia. Then I found out where the black neighborhoods, where people appreciated our low-cost merchandise, were in Boston, Cleveland, and Detroit.   3

I saved enough money to begin graduate school in NYU in September 1974. On weekends, and during vacations, I went on the road with friends, selling wigs throughout the eastern United States. We would take a bus to Buffalo, Detroit, Miami. Sometimes five of us would pile into a friend's car and go together. We'd carry an almanac with us. I'd   4 study the demographics of each neighborhood of the city we were approaching. I'd say, "This neighborhood is dangerous; we have to be careful. This area is more high-class, middle-class." After we visited an area, we had established customers, who would recognize us or be waiting for us to come back again.

We'd go to Albany, Syracuse, and Buffalo. Then we'd swing across   5 to Cleveland, Toledo, then Indiana and Detroit. We would just follow the road maps and the almanac. I had a Korean friend who was a professor in Miami. He lived there for fifteen years. But after one or two short peddling trips, I knew Miami better than him.

I would walk down a street and see someone having a party in their   6 backyard. They'd say, "We don't want to buy any wigs." I'd say, "Okay. I'll just rest here for a minute." I'd look around and choose the most beautiful lady. I'd go up to her and start to talk: "Whether you want to buy one or not, I'd like for you to try this new style one time." I'd take out a wig that was very beautiful. She'd shout, "Oh! That's beautiful." And all the people would come around and buy. [Laughs]

Sometimes men would buy for their wife or mother. Older people   7 saw us working all day, came to us, and said, "Why don't you come to my home and marry my daughter?" [Laughs] They saw how hard we worked and thought we'd make good husbands.

In the mornings I would go from store to store, from 9:00 A.M. until   8 mid-afternoon, collecting wholesale orders from merchants. I would telephone my wife in New York and tell her where to ship the orders. Then, around 4:00 P.M., I would peddle on the streets. I'd look for a good spot to sit and display my wigs. I'd earn $50 to $100. After sundown, my friends and I got into our car and drove to the next city.

Around 1:00 A.M. we'd stop at a roadside rest area to get a few hours'   9 sleep. We'd try to be in the next town by 9:00 A.M. Fridays, Saturdays, and Sundays were our best days. We'd be so busy that we couldn't talk or take time to eat. We saved a lot of money this way.

On a weekday, we might be on the highway between Toledo and   10 Columbus. I'd look in the almanac and see that we were approaching a big cigar factory. We'd pull into the factory parking lot at 5:00 P.M., when people were getting out of work, stand outside with our bags, and sell. Black ladies liked the wigs, because they don't have long straight hair. Most couldn't afford to buy a $300 or $400 human-hair wig. My wigs looked like human hair but only cost $10. They were made from a nylon material. The colors were black, red, all shades of brown. And older women liked mixed gray. Some women bought a few different colors to match their dresses.

In Indianapolis, we'd stand in front of a big hospial. Sometimes we'd   11
go right into the lobby and sell. A nurse would come by and say, "Okay, I want to buy a wig." They would go get their money and forget about their patients. Police would come by and check us. They said, "You can't work here. The nurses will get distracted, and their patients will all die."

One time we were standing on a sidewalk and people came by in a   12
long black car, going to a funeral. They stopped at a red light and came over to buy wigs.

When a policeman would check me out, I would show my New   13
York sales license. Sometimes that would be legal. But other times I had to purchase a permit at the local city hall. The prices varied from $3 to $60.

Sometimes we tried our luck in restricted areas. The police would   14
come by to warn us. The next time, angry, he'd say, "One more time and I'll send you all to jail." I'd say, "Officer, I'm a student. I don't have tuition. That's why I sell here." He'd look at me and say quietly, "Well, then, that's okay. You're a student. You can stay here except from ten until twelve." Sometimes the police helped us like that.

For us, time was money. And we had orders to fill. I would send the   15
money we earned to my wife with new order forms. She purchased the requested number and sent me two to three hundred wigs by UPS to a city where we were going to be in a few days. We asked her for as much merchandise as we could carry in our peddling bags. All the money we made, we reinvested to keep our business growing.

After a few months on the road, my business was established. A   16
group of Korean graduate students came to me in New York and asked me to teach them how to do business. They said, "You purchase the wigs wholesale, and we will buy from you for ourselves to sell." That's business, right? I named my company Dong Jin, "Going East," because I imported from Asia.

The students branched out to different cities. They'd go their separate   17
ways all over the United States. Each was responsible for their own peddling business. My wife and I only supplied them with merchandise. I was like the organizer of a group of businessmen. Now some are professors back in Korea, some are presidents of large companies, others work in the Korean government. And some are American citizens and doing quite well.

At first, my wife and I used our apartment as our warehouse and of-   18
fice. When we began to import wigs, business was brisk. Within four
months, I found a small office at 1261 Broadway, in the midtown business district. I would go out on the road selling while my wife ran the
warehouse.

Min Cha had to bring our three small children with her to the ware-   19
house. We didn't have anyone to babysit, but it was important to keep
the business going. She would walk up and down Broadway comparing
prices in different import and wholesale shops to find the best deal. We
knew some Korean importers and factories in the area. We could buy a
wig for 50¢ and sell it at a fair price for our friends to peddle.

Our children were only one, two, and three years old. Oh! my wife   20
had to take them everywhere with her! [Laughs] The babies would go
into the stores and play with everything.

Once we got our business going, we moved to Flushing, in Queens,   21
in 1976. Shortly after we moved, my wife's parents arrived from Korea.
Now, there are almost forty thousand Koreans living in Queens. Back
then the neighborhood was mostly Jewish. We found a nice apartment
with enough room for the kids, who were becoming pretty active.
When my wife's parents moved in with us, her mother helped with the
kids. That made things a lot easier.

Our home in Flushing was very near the subway to Manhattan. I read   22
newspapers and studied while riding to school. We didn't buy a car
until 1979. So, on wig-selling trips to different cities, I continued to use
the Greyhound bus, the Amtrak, or my friend's car. I had a lot of interesting experiences while peddling. One time I was able to learn a lot
about politics in this country.

Worcester, Massachusetts, was the home of Senator Edward Brooke,   23
who was the only black U.S. senator since the post–Civil War period.
He was on the Foreign Relations Committee. I went to his election campaign headquarters to ask questions about U.S.-Korea relations and to
see how they ran a campaign. About twenty or thirty women who
worked there told me that they wanted to buy wigs. I said, "No, I came
to see Senator Brooke." I spoke with some of the Senator's aides about
political situations. They liked me and said, "While you're doing your
wig selling, why don't you campaign for Brooke?" I said, "Okay." And
went house to house for Brooke. Thirty or forty people bought my wigs.
[Laughs]

I asked Brooke's aides many questions about how they handled the   24
Senator's re-election. Twenty or thirty campaigners for Brooke went into

a neighborhood to shake hands with people. I told the lady campaigners, "How about wearing a red wig? You'll look very beautiful." The staff bought wigs so they would look nice. And they taught me how to do a political campaign.

In some cities I would walk into the neighborhood bar. There would 25 be many people drinking, many ladies. I'd say, "Hello, ladies. Wigs for sale. I am a student trying to pay for my schooling." The owners of the bars were always black people. Sometimes people would say to me, "You go back to your own country." I said to them, "You go to your country. This is my country." They'd say, "You're Chinese. Why do you say this is your country?" I'd say, "Because I am an Indian. You're from Africa. This is my country. I'm not Chinese, I am American Indian." [Laughs]

I make a joke. But it's true that some American Indians came from 26 Manchuria and Korea centuries ago. They came across the Bering Strait into Alaska, then down the Canadian mountains into the United States. Look at Indian facial structures. They are very Oriental. Same eyes, same bone structure. Eskimos in Alaska, and Apache Indians and Koreans have some similar customs.

Once I met a man and said hello to him in Korean. He didn't under- 27 stand. I said to him, "You are not Korean?" He said, "No." I said, "Are you Chinese?" "No." "Japanese?" "No." "What are you?" He said, "American Indian."

One time I was in Detroit. My friend went into a bar to sell, and I 28 went into an apartment building. A man called, "Hey, Chinese." And he started going toward my friend with a gun. I saw him and said, "I know you want to rob my friend. We know kung fu. The Oriental custom is not to report to the police. If you try to rob us one more time, I will attack you."

In the Korean army we learned self-defense called "tae kwan do." 29 One or two robbers we could fight off. But if there were more than three with an ax or gun, no way. I was robbed many times—seven or eight times. In New York Harlem, dangerous areas of Detroit, Cleveland, Toledo, Richmond, Atlanta—people would come up to me with a gun and pull off my bag.

One time the robbers jumped into a car. It wouldn't start up for 30 them. I asked local residents if I could use their phone to call the police. The police wouldn't come. They were afraid of that neighborhood.

My first ten years in the United States, I never rested. I worked seven 31 days a week and studied, too. My teachers assigned us to read three to five hundred pages every week. It was very hard to keep up with my studies.

I finished graduate school at New York University in 1977. I was 32 forty-two years old and had no money saved: I spent everything on my education and taking care of my children. My wife was still developing the wholesale wig business, which was just successful enough to support my education. Because she put so much time into the business and caring for the children, she never re-entered her pharmacist profession.

I was very sad. Even though I finished my second master's degree, 33 after six years in the United States I still didn't have any money. I said, "All right, a master's degree is enough for me. Now I will establish myself." So I picked up the bag full of wigs and again began going door to door. In one or two days I made $200 or $300. My plan was for my wife and me to help ourselves by expanding our business. We could create very good jobs for students by peddling in their spare time.

I began to teach the students: "When you come into our wholesale 34 shop, we'll give you enough credit to sell for the week." Twenty or thirty students asked us, "Mr. Kim, if you import the products from Korea, we will buy at wholesale prices from you."

The plan began to work, and we were able to save and expand. In 35 1979, we moved our Dong Jin Trading Company into our current business building, on the corner of Broadway and West 29th Street. I didn't have the $10,000 necessary to put down on my store, so a friend cosigned for a bank loan. The space is a thousand square feet. With a twenty-foot ceiling, we were able to build a loft to use as our business office. And we have five hundred square feet in the basement for storage. There were four of us on our staff—my wife, her father, one employee, and me.

We would open in the mornings, at 8:00 A.M. At 7:00 P.M., we would 36 close the doors and begin packing the out-of-town orders until 1:00 A.M. or 3:00 A.M. We slept right in the store. Woke up at 6:00 A.M. and got back to work. After six months, we were making enough money to hire two more employees, including my wife's brother, who arrived from Korea.

We set up a small machine to make ladies' belts for wholesale. There 37 was a customer demand, and when we ordered belts from the factory, sometimes they couldn't deliver. So I said to my wife's father and brother, "Let's try to make our own belts downstairs. We can cut the cloth with scissors and sew on metal buckles."

The two of them worked all day long, producing around three dozen 38

belts each. We made around $1 on each belt. My brother-in-law be-
came frustrated. He told me: "Working like this, we'll never make any
money. I'm going to buy a cutting machine. This way we can produce
ten dozen belts per person each day."

When we earned back the money we spent on the machine, we   39
bought another. Soon we had three, four, five machines. The next step
was to rent another small space, in a building on West 31st Street, a few
blocks from our store, to be our factory. I went to the bank at least
twenty times trying to get a loan to improve the business. But they always refused. I said, "Okay, I must work harder."

Other Korean friends had the same experience with the banks, so we   40
decided to form our own credit union or investment corporation. We
each put $500 into one account, creating a seed fund of $8,000. Each
month we contributed to the fund. The account can be used to help finance projects of our membership or to make small loans to other people who would like to start their own business. As they continually paid
back the fund, the account continued to grow.

Enough Korean businesses were established that we developed asso-   41
ciations to help each other and introduce newcomers to the American
system. For example, I had two managers who worked at my shop for
four years. They were very faithful to me. I cosigned a bank loan so that
they could each have their own store. I've also helped four or five other
people find empty stores to buy in Brooklyn, Harlem, or the Bronx. I enjoyed helping these people to become independent.

Rent is a serious problem for any businesses in Manhattan. In Korea,   42
rents go up at most ten percent in a year. But in New York City, a store
owner can lose his business because of skyrocketing [increases]. Some
rents in this area have jumped from $1,000 a month to more than
$10,000 in just five years.

Around sixty-five percent of Koreans in New York work in Korean-   43
owned small or middle-size businesses, either as the owner or employees. On both sides of Broadway, between 25th and 34th Streets, more
than half the stores are owned by Koreans.

In the building where our store is housed, we are still renting. But   44
some friends and I pooled our money and bought another building in
this neighborhood. One of my friends manages that building, where five
or six companies rent offices. Step by step, I've learned to invest our
money and still have enough to manage the import-export business effi-
ciently.

The products we sell come in large quantity from Korea, Taiwan, 45
China, Japan. Large shipments come into the warehouse every week.
We use a small computer to make our orders and determine how much
we need. My wife handles most of the day-to-day management.

In the factory we have stacks and stacks of materials that we cut into 46
belts: cloth, leather, plastics. We use different machines in an assembly
line: cutting, stamping holes, inserting buckles. We've hired a dozen
people now to make belts and do the stock work. Some are Vietnamese,
some are Chinese. They work only one shift, from 8:00 A.M. until 4:00
P.M. My father manages the factory and watches over the warehouse.
We have ten thousand square feet full of merchandise. You can see
three hundred different types of items piled to the ceiling. Long boxes
from Japan contain scarves. Stacks of square boxes are full of gloves
from Taipei. Hats from Korea . . . We need to expand into a larger warehouse.

I go on business trips throughout Asia to establish contacts with the 47
trade agencies who ship products to my store. My customers tell me the
types of items and volumes they need; then I place the orders. Many of
my customers have small retail shops in poor neighborhoods, so we
make sure the items we import can be sold inexpensively. Rhinestone
costume jewelry we carry can be sold retail for $2 or $3. Sunglasses,
gloves, baseball caps are all under $5 or $10. During Christmas, we sell
a lot of small toys.

We ship orders to many states. I have good contacts throughout the 48
East Coast and Midwest from when I was a peddler in all those cities.
And some of our orders go to South America, Canada, even to Africa.
We ship mostly by airplane, but you'd be surprised—people come in
from as far away as Canada to buy in large quantities.

During the course of a year, we are doing around $4–5 million worth 49
of transactions. We make a five- to six-percent net profit on that
amount. We have to pay the overhead on our store, taxes, salaries for
our workers, and other expenses.

A number of our clients in Manhattan are West Indian merchants 50
and Africans who peddle on the streets, as well as Korean shopowners.
We have to open early, because some clients like to come in before
they open their shops. Others like to come in after they close shop. So
we seldom leave the store before 7:00 or 8:00 P.M., and we still get up
for work at 5:30 A.M.

In 1982, we moved to Paramus, New Jersey, a suburban area. After 51 ten years of always working, studying, and taking care of the family, my business had become more successful. I thought that I could finally start to get a little more rest on weekends. At that time, my son, John, was in the fifth grade. He wanted to take a job delivering newspapers to save money for his education. I said, "Okay, good idea." Then he said to me, "Sunday is a very big day for newspapers. Father, you must help me by driving the car." [Laughs]

   I've come full circle. When I was in middle school in Korea, I began   52
delivering papers. And thirty-five years later, I am delivering newspapers again [laughs] with my boy.

. . . .

RESPONSE AND ANALYSIS

1. Write for a few minutes in response to what you have read. Besides summarizing, you may want to explore your feelings and thoughts about the reading. It may be helpful to consider these categories:

   a. what you understood about the reading

   b. something that puzzled you in the reading

   c. something you would like to discuss with the writer, the interviewee, or one of the characters

   d. a memory the reading evoked

   e. how you felt about the reading

2. Make a list of the major events in Kim's life here in the United States. Then put the list in *chronological,* or time, order.

3. Kim relates several interesting anecdotes from his days on the road. Briefly summarize these.

4. How have the other members of the Kim family contributed to the success of the business?

5. Apart from the many details related to building his business, what other themes does Kim discuss in the interview?

. . . .

FURTHER EXPLORATION OF LANGUAGE AND LITERATURE: USING MAPS

You've seen how important it is to continuously investigate the historical, cultural, and literary references you come across in your reading. As you accumulate more knowledge of the world, you will read with fuller comprehension and enjoy the experience more.

Are you familiar with the many American cities Kim mentions as he talks about his days on the road? To build your knowledge of geography, it is a good idea to refer to a map and locate the cities, states, and countries you come across in your reading.

1. Make a list of the cities Kim visited on his peddling trips.

2. Using a road map of the United States (you can find one at any library if you don't have one), locate the cities that Kim mentions. What *itinerary* or route would a traveling salesman follow if he wanted to cover these cities on one trip? On two or more trips?

Student Essay

For her essay about work experiences, Ana Villa from the Dominican Republic chose to interview her mother, Lucía. (The interview was conducted in Spanish.) Although Ana's mother had worked for many years in her homeland, Ana focused exclusively on her mother's work experiences in the United States.

AN AMBITIOUS WORKER

ANA VILLA

Unfortunately, it's not uncommon to see Latinos in my neighborhood working in a factory for many years. However, there are exceptions. There are those who go from a low-paying job to a better one, while going to school in order to move on to an even better position. My mother Lucía is such an example. She first worked as a sewing machine operator making sweaters. Now she is working in the health care field as a home attendant. However, she is still not satisfied and plans to continue her education to study nursing or social work.

My mother's first job here in the United States was in a factory sewing sweaters. "I didn't like that job at all. I worked five long days a week for only $270," she said bitterly. She added that the job offered no fringe benefits. "It was a hard job. I had to wake up very early to go to a dirty job. I was always removing wool from my nose," she recalled.

There are five children in the family and the salary wasn't high enough. Although my father is a plumber, he works on his own. There are certain times when there is no work. A friend told her about working as a home attendant. My mother began to train for the position: "I took four days of classes where I learned about nutrition and how to treat the elderly. I learned about the most frequent illnesses of the elderly and what to do in case of an emergency." After the training my mother passed an examination and received the license to work as a home attendant.

As opposed to her first job, her current position provides benefits. My 4 mother spoke with satisfaction in her voice when she said, "They pay me holidays, sick days, vacations, and I earn more than before." She is paid $7.60 an hour and has the opportunity to work seven days a week if she wants to earn extra money.

Her duties in this job revolve around taking care of elderly people 5 who live alone. Many are sick. She has to take them to the doctor and run errands for them, such as going shopping. The pride my mother felt was obvious when she said, "A home attendant means a lot to old-aged people. They're scared of strangers and they look upon their home attendant as part of their family."

She spoke of some of her clients. One who was 60 years old suffered 6 from high blood pressure and diabetes. The saddest case was a man who was only 40 years old but had cancer. Currently she has a patient who has Alzheimer's disease. According to my mother, this is very difficult to deal with: "She is not well in her mind. She talks to herself and doesn't know what she is doing."

Despite the advantages over her previous job, my mother hopes to 7 move on. She is attending Hostos Community College, taking courses in nursing. Back home in the Dominican Republic she worked as a volunteer in the local hospital. She is also considering social work. Her work as a home attendant, where she has dealt with people who are not well, should prove helpful in either of those careers.

My mother is full of hope for the future: "I will work as a nurse or a 8 social worker and things will be better." I am proud of her. She serves as an example to me, to Latinos, and all immigrants who come to the United States.

. . . .

RESPONSE AND ANALYSIS

1. What sort of woman is Lucía? Bring specific evidence from the essay to support your description.

2. Discuss the advantages and disadvantages of the various jobs Lucía has had.

3. In a number of places in the essay, Ana has used direct quotations from the interview. For example, in paragraph 2, she writes that her mother says, "I didn't like
   that job at all. I worked five long days a week for only $270." Ana then switches to re-
   ported speech, with her mother's remarks about the lack of fringe benefits. Compile
   two lists: one for examples of direct quotations and one for examples of reported
   speech. What factors did Ana consider when deciding to use one or the other?

4. When we speak, we communicate meaning not only through words but also
   through nonverbal clues such as facial expressions, tone of voice, and body language. In paragraph 4, for example, Ana observes that her mother spoke "with
   satisfaction in her voice." Where else has Ana included observations about nonverbal communication?

5. Before Ana wrote her essay, she prepared an outline to help her organize her
   notes. Try to reconstruct the outline Ana used by identifying the main idea of
   each paragraph and the topic sentence, if one is used.

Focus on Writing: Interviewing

In generating ideas for the essays you have written to this point, you have not
needed to gather information outside of your own personal experiences. Sometimes,
however, you will want to supplement your own experiences with information and
ideas from other sources. As a first step, you may want to begin by talking with your
acquaintances. Later, you will probably want to go to books, newspapers and periodicals, and even films and recordings to research your topic. Keep in mind that if you
have been investigating the various references you have encountered in your reading, you have been doing research all along!

The essay you will be asked to write in this chapter will be based on an interview
you conduct. Obviously, the quality of your essay will depend directly on your interview experience. You may find it easy to talk and socialize with people, but interviewing requires some effort. You must choose the themes you intend to focus on in
the interview, prepare a list of questions, and of course, record the responses of your
subject. Later you must organize the responses for your essay.

. . . .

QUESTIONING

Most professional interviewers on television and the radio, or in newspapers or magazines, would emphasize the importance of planning for a successful interview, in-

cluding the preparation of the questions. As you get ready to do your interview, keep in mind the themes you want to focus on and prepare your questions accordingly. For example, in her interview, Ana Villa knew that she wanted to focus on her mother's experiences working in the United States. Her preparation included writing questions such as:

What was your first job here in the United States?

What were the working conditions?

What other jobs have you had?

Based on the essay Ana has written, what other questions do you think she prepared for the interview?

Many of the issues you explored as you generated ideas for your own essays will help you prepare questions for your interview. For example, suppose you wanted to generate ideas about an incident caused by your limited English. You may have asked yourself specific questions, such as where and when the incident happened, what were the results of your inability to communicate effectively, how you felt, what you learned from the experience, and how you feel about the incident today. In contrast, a question such as "Was it hard to learn English?" is so broad that it may only elicit a short yes-or-no response.

While preparation is important for a successful interview, you must also be *flexible,* that is, able to change in order to adapt to new or unforeseen circumstances. The responses of your subject may lead you to topics you hadn't anticipated. Ana's mother, in her responses to questions about her work experiences, mentions items that Ana could not have known beforehand. As a skilled interviewer, however, Ana asks appropriate follow-up questions. For example, when her mother mentions that she went through a four-day training period in order to become a home attendant, it is obvious that Ana followed up by asking a question such as, "What sorts of things were covered in the training?"

Based on the essay Ana has written, what other follow-up questions do you think she asked in order to explore her mother's responses in greater detail?

· · · · · · · · · · · · · · · · ·

NOTE TAKING

Of course, during the interview you have to record the responses of your subject to use later in your essay. If you plan on using a tape recorder, it is a good idea to try out the machine before the interview. If you do not use a tape recorder, you will have to be particularly good at taking notes as your subject speaks. Obviously, your subject will speak faster than you can write. To help you take notes during the interview, keep these points in mind:

1. Jot down key words and phrases, as if you were taking notes in a classroom. It is not necessary to write complete sentences. Use abbreviations whenever possible.

2. Although you will later relate most of what your subject says through reported speech, try to write down a number of meaningful direct quotations.

3. Don't forget to note significant examples of nonverbal communication such as tone of voice, facial expressions, and body language.

4. If your interview is conducted in a language other than English, take your notes in that language. You can translate later.

Afterward you will have to decide how to organize your notes into an essay. Freewriting about the interview and/or preparing an outline from your notes is usually helpful.

Many students find it helpful to engage in a practice interview in class before going out "into the field." You may feel more at ease working with someone who has the same assignment. A practice session can give you the opportunity to be both interviewer and subject. In addition, you can get some immediate feedback from your classmates and teacher.

Claude St. Vil from Haiti wrote the following essay based on his in-class interview with classmate Claritza Gálvez from Ecuador. Later, Claude was interviewed by another student in the class.

A WHOLE NEW WORLD

CLAUDE ST. VIL

Claritza Gálvez came to the United States from Ecuador on January 19, 1989. She was surprised by what awaited her. In Ecuador she thought that New York was a beautiful clean city where people found "money on the streets." Consequently, Claritza was shocked when she saw the filthy streets of her Brooklyn neighborhood and old burned-down buildings in some parts of the Bronx. She also learned soon that her notions about the easy money were false as well. Claritza's father has to work long hours in his small restaurant to support his family.

Before leaving Ecuador, Claritza was both excited and sad. She knew that she was going to leave her friends and family. On the other hand, she wanted to be reunited with her father, who had come to the United States five years earlier to prepare a home and everything necessary for a comfortable life for his family. When I asked her how she felt the first months in a foreign country, she said with sadness in her eyes, "Sometimes I wished I had never come here." However, her face quickly brightened as she explained to me that now after a number of years being here in the United States, she has gotten used to American customs and has met a lot of friends. She seems to be genuinely happy.

I was also interested in Claritza's experiences in her new school and her new friends. She told me that she was very surprised when she came to high school for the first time and she noticed that so many students spoke Spanish, her native language. As a result she was able to find a lot of friends very quickly. Also, she didn't have many traumatic experiences in school because she had the opportunity to go to a bilingual program where her science, social studies, and mathematics classes were all taught in Spanish.   3

When I asked Claritza what surprised her the most about schools here, she shrugged her shoulders and said, "The relationship between teacher and students in school for me was hard to understand." Claritza used to go to strict schools in Ecuador. All the students had respect for their teachers. They even wore uniforms. Therefore, when she saw how often students speak disrespectfully to the teachers here, she was amazed and alarmed. She was also surprised by the way her classmates dressed: the uniforms had been replaced by colorful, often strange styles of clothing.   4

At the end of our talk, I asked Claritza if she was happy living in New York and if she was considering going back to Ecuador. Despite the differences between her country and the United States, Claritza has adapted to life here and will probably stay here. Her children will be Americans.   5

. . . .

RESPONSE AND ANALYSIS

1. Which main themes did Claude choose to focus on in his essay about Claritza?

2. As you have seen, a successful interview involves preparing questions as well as asking follow-up questions to your subject's responses. Based on Claude's essay, try to figure out the questions he asked during his interview. Make two categories: *prepared questions* and *follow-up questions*. Put the questions you think Claude asked in the appropriate category.

3. Like Ana, before Claude wrote his essay he prepared an outline. Try to reconstruct the outline Claude used by identifying the main idea of each paragraph and the topic sentence, if one is used.

4. Where has Claude included direct quotations? Reported speech? Observations about nonverbal communication?

5. A number of times in the essay Claude refers to the interview process. For example, in paragraph 2 he writes, "When I asked her how she felt the first months in a foreign country. . . . " Where else does Claude do this? Do you like this technique of making reference to the interview process? Explain.

You've already seen the importance of being flexible during your interview so that you can explore topics that you hadn't planned on. In his in-class interview, Eric Guzmán, whose essay "Riding on a Lonely Train" appears in chapter 1, planned to cover the kinds of topics Claude had covered: first impressions of the United States, school, family, and the future. However, when his subject, José, mentioned that he had entered the United States illegally, Eric was flexible enough to abandon his prepared questions. He continued to inquire about José's experiences as an illegal immigrant. This became the primary focus of the interview and the subsequent essay.

An Interview with an Illegal Immigrant

ERIC GUZMÁN

After I interviewed my classmate José, I understood how difficult it is   1
to be an illegal immigrant here in the United States. I am an immigrant also but I came here the easy way: on a comfortable plane with a visa from Honduras. My friend José had to travel over land from El Salvador, crossing two countries to reach the United States. He reached New York but because he is here illegally, his problems continue.

"I decided to come to the United States because I wanted to help my   2
sisters in El Salvador. There were a lot of troubles there with the civil war. You never knew if you were going to wake up the next day," José began. He told me that his mother was killed by guerrillas and that his father abandoned him and his sisters shortly thereafter.

I asked him how he got the money to travel all the way here. José re-   3
sponded, "My friend gave me some money that he had collected by selling a rifle he had found. Also I worked for some time in a supermarket and I was able to save money." He left El Salvador with only 200 colones—about 25 American dollars. After he had traveled for a day by bus, he reached the border with Guatemala. By telling the border guards that he had come for a short pleasure trip, he was permitted to

enter Guatemala. He found work there and was able to save enough money to continue his trip.

José's problems began in Mexico: "I was in Mexico for only a month, but it seemed like a year. The first day there the police took my money and told me that if I said anything they would send me back to the bloodshed of my country. I didn't know how they had learned that I was not Mexican and that I was trying to cross the border illegally." He was stranded without money and with no place to stay. He had nothing to eat.   4

"Looking for a job was the hardest part," José continued. "Nobody wanted to give me work. They said that the Central Americans come to Mexico to take away the jobs that belong to Mexicans. They blamed their own poverty on the influx of illegal immigrants from El Salvador and Guatemala."   5

Finally José found a job working as a security guard in a grocery store. Here his adventures continued: "One night two robbers entered the store. I called the owner and he called the police. When the police arrived, I had to hide because if they saw me, they would deport me." After three weeks of working, José had enough money to continue his journey northward.   6

When asked what he thinks of the people he had met in Mexico, José looked up and breathed deeply. He spoke slowly: "As with any group of people, I believe that most are good; some are not. Most people in Mexico were very nice to me and they help those in need. But a few were very bad and instead of helping the illegals, they called the police."   7

José crossed the border with the United States with the help of a *coyote*. A coyote is a person who helps Mexicans and Central and South Americans sneak into the United States. He paid the coyote $100 to get him to the other side. He swam across the Rio Grande and took a truck with other people to Brownsville, Texas, where he worked on a farm for two weeks. There too he had to hide from the immigration police. Twice they raided the farm looking for illegal workers.   8

José's ultimate destination was New York, where he had an aunt. "I called her and asked her to send me the bus fare so I could come here. I promised to pay her back when I got a job. She soon sent me $150. You can imagine how happy I was to see her waiting for me when I got off the bus in the Port Authority Bus Terminal on 42nd Street in Manhattan. When I was settled in her home, she told me that I was not going to work, that I was going to go to school. At first I refused the offer but I realized   9 that if I didn't have an education I would never be able to improve my status here and help my sisters." In a few days, José was in school.

Still, because of his illegal status here, life is hard. He is not able to find a job because he must provide a social security number, which of course he doesn't have. He also feels sad because he is unable to go back to his country.   10

After the interview I realized that there are thousands of people like José. People who have done incredibly difficult, dangerous, and brave things to come to the United States in order to improve their lives. Many are disappointed because they are unable to improve their position in life because of their illegal status. More than that, always in their minds are their loved ones and the life they left behind.   11

. . . .

RESPONSE AND ANALYSIS

1. How have José's experiences and status as an illegal immigrant affected his life? Do you know anyone who has gone through the same thing? In what ways do experiences such José's affect a person?

2. Make four categories: *El Salvador, Guatemala, Mexico,* and the *United States.* List the experiences that José relates in the appropriate category.

3. Try to reconstruct the outline Eric used to help him organize his notes by identifying the main idea of each paragraph and the topic sentence, if one is used.

4. Where has Eric included direct quotations? Reported speech? Observations about nonverbal communication? References to the interview process?

Essay Writing

. . . .

GENERATING IDEAS

The essay you are asked to write in this chapter will be based on an interview you conduct with someone about his or her experiences in the world of work. The quality of the material you generate for your essay will depend directly on the interview. (You probably will want to do a practice interview in class.) To help you conduct a successful interview, keep the following points in mind:

- Decide on the theme(s) you plan to focus on and prepare your questions beforehand.

- Your prepared questions are important, but be sure to ask appropriate follow-up questions.

- Remember that the goal of the interview is to elicit interesting and meaningful material. Ask questions that will encourage your subject to respond.

- Be flexible if topics you hadn't anticipated arise.

- To help you take notes—even if you are using a tape recorder—jot down key words or phrases and use abbreviations.

- After the interview, freewrite about the experience and/or prepare an outline to help you organize your notes.

. . . .

ASSIGNMENT

Use your freewriting and/or outline as the basis of an essay about your subject's experiences in the world of work. Keep in mind the elements Ana, Claude, and Eric have included in their successful essays: the use of direct quotation and reported speech, observations about nonverbal communication, and references to the interview process. After you have written an early draft of your essay, share it with a classmate. Use the section "Review: Elements of the Essay" in the previous chapter as you engage in peer revision to make your essay even more successful.

ISSUES
IN THE NEWS

. . . .

Many teachers believe that the most important thing a student of English can do is read a newspaper every day. Which current issues in the news do you find of particular interest?

READING

Teach Your Children Well

PAUL GRAY

. . . .

ESTABLISHING THE CONTEXT

The rise in immigration to the United States has underscored the need for school districts to establish a policy on how to educate students with language backgrounds other than English. Essentially two approaches have been considered: bilingual education and immersion into instruction entirely in English. Bilingual education provides students with the opportunity to study their native language and culture while receiving instruction in ESL (English as a Second Language). Many bilingual programs offer content area subjects such as social studies, mathematics, and science in languages other than English. In contrast, in immersion programs students with limited English take classes with their English-speaking schoolmates, often receiving supplementary ESL instruction.

Although many Americans think of bilingual education as a relatively recent phenomenon, there is a long history of public schools in the United States offering instruction in languages other than English. As early as 1840, German-English bilingual education was provided in the public schools of Cincinnati, Ohio. The scope of bilingual education has increased dramatically in the last few decades, supported by the federal government and the courts. The Bilingual Education Act of 1968 allocated federal funds to meet the special educational needs of students with limited English. In 1974 the Supreme Court declared in the Lau vs. Nichols case that Asian students in San Francisco had been denied equal educational opportunity due to their inability to speak and understand English. A result of the decision was to deny federal funds to school districts that do not address the needs of such students.

Despite the growth of bilingual education in the United States, or perhaps because of it, the issue remains controversial. Well-intentioned people have come to very different conclusions on the most effective way to educate students with language backgrounds other than English. This is explored in "Teach Your Children Well." The article comes from a special issue of the national news magazine *Time*, devoted entirely to the recent immigrant experience of the United States.

. . . .

TO BEGIN

1. Read the first three paragraphs of the selection. Notice how the article develops:

Paragraph 1: A specific anecdote about a first-grade class in New York City with students who were not born in the United States.

Paragraph 2: A general statement about the recent rise in immigration to the United States and its effect on the country's educational system.

Paragraph 3: Specific factual information about the increase in the number of students in American public schools who speak languages other than English.

As you continue reading, you will see that the article contains material in the form of anecdotes, facts, explanations, and opinions. Later you will be able to analyze this material in greater detail.

2. The article contains a number of difficult technical words and phrases related to the theme of how to educate the children of immigrants. Brainstorm ideas about the significance of each phrase below and how it might relate to the theme explored in the article. To facilitate your discussion, you may want to refer to an English-English or bilingual dictionary.

   tural dissonance

   pragmatic methods

   ethnic diversity

   Eurocentric bias

   cultural identity

   budgetary restraints and cutbacks

   recession and fiscal crisis

   bureaucracy

   dwindling resources

As you read the article, check to see if you were able to anticipate the significance of these words and phrases to the themes explored in the piece.

There will probably be other unfamiliar words in "Teach Your Children Well." Remember, however, that you can still enjoy and understand what you read without knowing the definition of every word. Try to use the context to guess at the unfamiliar words and phrases as you read for your interest and pleasure about the education of students with limited English. Don't be overly concerned with words and phrases you don't understand; after you read, respond to, and analyze the article, there will be an individualized vocabulary activity in which you will be asked to choose other words that you found challenging.

TEACH YOUR CHILDREN WELL

What to Teach the Newest Arrivals in What Language Still Vexes
the Nation's Public Schools

PAUL GRAY

On a cloudy winter afternoon, Florann Greenberg, a teacher at P.S. 14   1
in New York City, noticed that her first-grade class was growing fidgety. One girl, dropping all pretense of work, stared at the snow falling out-side the schoolroom windows. Annoyed, Greenberg asked her, "Haven't you seen snow before?" The girl whispered, "No." Her class-mates began shaking their heads. Then it dawned on Greenberg: *of course* these children had never seen snow; almost all were immigrants from Colombia and the Dominican Republic. Immediately, she changed the lesson plan. New topic: What is snow? How is it formed? How do you dress in the snow? What games do you play?

Such moments of cultural dissonance, followed by attempts to learn   2
and teach from them, now take place daily in thousands of classrooms scattered across the U.S. The children of the new immigrants, often im-migrants themselves, have been arriving at these classrooms in growing numbers, and more are on the way. They are placing unprecedented demands on teachers, administrators and already strained school sys-tems. To a heartening degree, however, educators are responding with fresh, pragmatic methods of coping with these new demands.

Isolated numbers hint at the scope of the challenge: 3

* Total enrollment in U.S. public schools rose only 4.2% between 1986   4
  and 1991, according to a 1993 Urban Institute study, while the num-ber of students with little or no knowledge of English increased 50%, from 1.5 million to 2.3 million.

* In the Washington school system, students speak 127 languages and   5
  dialects; across the Potomac, in Fairfax County, Virginia, that figure is more than 100.

* In California public schools 1 out of 6 students was born outside the U.S.,   6
  and 1 in 3 speaks a language other than English at home. The Los Angeles school system now absorbs 30,000 new immigrant children each year.

Such figures, startling as they are, have stirred little national atten-   7
tion, in part because the new immigrant families have not spread themselves uniformly across the country. A recent Rand Corp. study found
that 78% of school-age immigrants who have been in the U.S. three
years or less live in just five states: California, New York, Texas, Florida
and Illinois. Like most statistics, this one can be misleading if it is taken
to mean that the surge of immigrant students is solely a big-state, big-
city concern. In absolute terms, even a small number of such students can profoundly affect the way a school district goes about its business.

In Garden City, Kansas (pop. 24,600), a boom in the meat-packing   8
industry that began during the 1980s continues to attract aspiring workers, principally from Mexico and Southeast Asia. Now, of the 3,666
children in Garden City's elementary schools, roughly 700 require special help because of limited proficiency in English. Lowell, Massachusetts, was a fading city of 19th century textile mills until 1985, when the
Federal Government chose it as a resettlement site for Southeast Asian
families. This year, aided by federal and state grants, Lowell spent $5.9
million on bilingual education; courses are offered in Spanish, Khmer,
Lao, Portuguese and Vietnamese. All communications between schools
and parents are translated into five languages. At the Cary Reynolds elementary school in the Atlanta suburb of De Kalb County, Georgia, students from 25 foreign nations speak a medley of languages ranging from
Mandarin to Farsi.

In practice, many teachers have begun turning the problems of eth-   9
nic diversity in their classrooms to educational advantage. Most elementary schools in Garden City celebrate different national holidays, including Mexican Independence Day, the Laotian New Year and
Vietnam's Tet. Last year a class at New York City's P.S. 189, which is
roughly one-third Haitian, performed a class project about Jean-Jacques
Dessalines, the slave who freed Haiti from France. The exercise was
consistent with both Haitian cultural traditions and the school's emphasis on maintaining harmony and diversity.

But the nation's school systems are not being swept by the kind of   10
wholesale changes that traditionalists feared would result from such
programs as New York City's controversial "Children of the Rainbow"
curriculum and Portland, Oregon's baseline essays, which aim to re-
duce the perceived Eurocentric bias of U.S. education. The ideological
debate about multicultural education, brewing for years on college
campuses, does not seem to have leached into primary and secondary

schools, where math, science, geography, etc., are still regarded as important. Nonetheless, vexing but essential questions prevail: How are students who know no English to be taught? Must they, in the process, sacrifice their ethnic or cultural heritage?

Surprisingly, most educators who work with the new immigrants believe competence in English and the maintenance of cultural identity are compatible goals. "I believe in language and cultural pride," says Martin Gross, a New York City elementary school principal, "but let's not forget the fact that these kids are in America. I think we should respect different cultures but not become factionalized." Claudia Hammock, a teacher at the Cary Reynolds school, agrees: "We do try to keep their native customs and try to show them we want them to remember. But we also want them to learn to function in an English-speaking world."   11

To reach that goal, teachers and administrators have, over several years of trial and error, evolved two different methods. In one, students are plunged immediately into intensive E.S.L. (English as a Second Language) instruction; the idea is to bring them up to the proficiency of native speakers at their grade level and get them into mainstream classes as quickly as possible. The other, bilingual, approach allows students to take courses such as math and history in their own languge while devoting a certain amount of time each day to learning English. Once the new language has been mastered, the students can translate and build upon their earlier, non-English instruction.   12

Both techniques have proved appealing to students. Carol Ovndo, 12, arrived in Fairfax County from Guatemala three years ago without knowing a word of English. Her immersion in all-English courses rapidly enabled her to become a proficient speaker and reader. "It was scary," she recalls. "But my teacher showed me pictures, and my friends helped, and sometimes we just all acted things out." At the Bell Multi-Cultural High School in Washington, Nguyen Nguyen, 15, who arrived from Vietnam a year ago, takes courses in both his native language and English. "I have to understand in Vietnamese first," he says, "so I can translate it into English. I learn best this way."   13

Both techniques have their drawbacks. English-only works better for younger students but can prove too rigorous for older children, who may grow frustrated and disinterested in school as a result. Children who live in families and communities where a foreign language is spoken often take so long to master English that they lack basic factual knowledge once they enter mainstream courses.   14

Most teachers now prefer the bilingual method. Says Winnie Porter,   15
a bilingual teacher at the Cesar Chavez Elementary School in San Francisco: "It's very simple. You teach children in the language they think
in; then they understand the concepts. Once they understand the concepts, they can transfer these skills to a second language. I know it
works. I've been doing it for 10 years and see the results." But many
communities cannot afford or attract qualified bilingual teachers in all—
or any—of the subjects students may need. Says Gloria McDonell, di-
rector of the Fairfax County E.S.L. program: "We don't teach bilingual
education because it's impractical. It's hard to find someone who can
teach math in Korean."

Unfortunately, the task of immigrant education occurs at a time   16
when the budgetary restraints and cutbacks in American public schools
are pinching resources for all students, native-born or otherwise. Immigration policy is made at the federal level, but the costs of educating the
children must be largely borne by financially beleaguered states and
municipalities. More than 65,000 immigrant children entered New York
City schools from April 1992 to April 1993, arriving in a system whose
budget has been reduced by more than three-quarters of a billion dollars since 1990. California's recession and fiscal crisis produced a 20%
drop in school funding between 1990 and 1992.

Donald Huddle, an economics professor at Rice University, has stud-   17
ied the expenses incurred by the 11.8 million legal and illegal immigrants in the U.S. in 1992. Out of a total $42.5 billion bill paid by all
levels of government, the largest line item was for primary and secondary education: $13.2 billion. Assuming an additional 11.1 million
new immigrants will come to the U.S. during the next decade, Huddle
predicts that the net cost will be $668.5 billion. If these figures are accu-
rate, they will be enough to bankrupt most school districts.

Can the U.S. afford to educate immigrants, especially at a time when   18
American students are testing poorly in a whole battery of subjects compared with their counterparts in other industrialized nations? Some crit-
ics vehemently think not. "Many schools with influxes of immigrant
children with specific educational needs weren't coping well to begin
with," says Ira Mehlman of the Federation for American Immigration
Reform, a group promoting immigration restrictions. "You can't keep
throwing these types of children into a school system and expect us to
have an educated population that will be competitive in this society."
Anthony Martin, a Palm Beach attorney and Republican gubernatorial

candidate in Florida, concurs: "Hundreds of millions of dollars are being stolen from American children who need computers, books and guards."

Yet even those who agree with such sentiments must concede that the immigrant children are already here; ignoring them, turning them away at the schoolhouse door for lack of money or will, is not just against the American character, it is against the law. The challenges their presence creates are real enough. So is the sense that no central authority has made itself responsible for these children's support, education and future prospects in society. Lorraine M. McDonnell, a consultant at the Rand Corp. who co-authored its recent report on immigrants in schools, recalls, "What we found is that, at the local level, schools and individuals are doing the best they can. The immigrant children are eager and hardworking, and teachers love to teach them. But they are not getting the assistance they need." 19

If there is a potential silver lining in these prognoses, it is that the initiatives and experiments now being demanded of individual schools, teachers and administrators may spark a long-needed rejuvenation in U.S. education. The dead hand of bureaucracy has not yet grasped the teaching of immigrants or clamped down on classroom innovations. For the moment, teachers of such children need not file proposed changes in lesson plans, in triplicate, to the board of ed offices and then wait six months to have the papers returned, stamped INSUFFICIENT INFORMATION. Constrained only by the number of hours in each working day, they are dealing with immigrants as individuals, using different approaches to meet different abilities and expectations. 20

Interestingly, those on the front lines of this struggle—the teachers and the local administrators burdened by growing responsibilities and dwindling resources—have hardly any complaints about the new immigrants. "We have had to create new programs and courses quickly," says Fairfax County's McDonell. "There have been problems. But slowly and surely, this is helping us understand what the rest of the world is like." Donna Skinner, at Garden City Community College, has worked closely with immigrant children in southwestern Kansas since 1980. "You're always going to find some people grumbling about special needs, but there is a certain pride here," she says. "This adds color and zest to our community." Says Lowell superintendent George Tsapatsaris: "If our country is going to compete globally in Southeast Asia, we need to have people who can speak those languages. My kids from Lowell will be in good shape." 21

Having embarked on the large-scale education of new immigrant   22
children, the U.S. has no choice but to continue on a journey toward a
distant if problematic destination. One of the surprise lessons along the
way may be that these young people, from virtually every spot on earth,
may have as much to teach as they have to learn.

Should it be the duty of all immigrants to learn English if they plan to stay in this country?

. . . .

Yes	No
96%	**4%**

From a telephone poll of 1,108 adult Americans taken for TIME/CNN on Sept. 8–9 by
Yankelovich Partners Inc. Sampling error is ±3%.

Which comes closest to your views on bilingual education in public schools?

. . . .

Teach children of immigrants in their native language
indefinitely.   **11%**

. . . .

Teach children of immigrants in their native language
only until they know enough English to join regular
classes.   **48%**

. . . .

Teach all children in English.   **40%**

. . . .

RESPONSE AND ANALYSIS

1. Write for a few minutes in response to what you have read. Besides
   summarizing, you may want to explore your feelings and thoughts
   about the reading. It may be helpful to consider these categories:

   a. what you understood about the reading

   b. something that puzzled you in the reading

   c. something you would like to ask the writers or one of the people
      mentioned in the article

   d. a memory the reading evoked

   e. how you felt about the reading

2. The article discusses two methods of educating immigrant children
   with limited English: immersion into English instruction and the

bilingual approach. The advantages and disadvantages of each are discussed. Summarize these.

3. Prepare an outline for the article in which you identify the main theme of each paragraph and the topic sentence, if one is used.

4. An *opinion poll* is a method of finding out the opinion of a population about an issue by questioning a relatively small number of people selected at random. Polling is an important technique employed by news organizations, and you will often come across references to opinion polls in newspapers and magazines. The article from *Time* cites the results of a recent opinion poll in which two questions were asked. Explain the poll results included in the article. Then indicate how you would have responded had you been part of this poll, and explain why would you have responded this way.

5. Has this article affected your position on the topic? Explain.

· · · · · · · · · · · · · · · · ·

FURTHER EXPLORATION OF LANGUAGE AND LITERATURE: FACT VS. OPINION

Consider the statement, "In California public schools 1 out of 6 students was born outside the U. S., and one in three speaks a language other than English." This is a *fact* that can be confirmed by checking information gathered by the United States Census Bureau as well as by other local and state agencies. In contrast, a statement in favor of bilingual education, such as, "You [should] teach children in the language they think in," is an *opinion.* As you have seen, how to educate students with language backgrounds other than English is a controversial issue on which people disagree.

Pay particular attention to statements that are written as if they were facts if no supporting evidence is provided. For example, consider the statement, "Most teachers now prefer the bilingual method." This may be a fact supported by the results of opinion polls and other kinds of research. However, if the supporting evidence is not cited, it is impossible to know if it is true.

As a careful reader, you must be able to distinguish between statements of *fact* and statements of *opinion,* as well as recognize statements that appear to be factual but are unsupported. This is particularly important when you are dealing with controversial issues.

The statements below are from the article "Teach Your Children Well." Determine if each statement is a *fact,* an *opinion,* or if it is *impossible to judge* based on the information provided. Afterward, discuss your answers with a classmate. You might find that not everybody has come to the same conclusions!

1. In the Washington school system, students speak 127 languages and dialects.

2. In absolute terms, even a small number of such students can profoundly affect the way a school district goes about its business.

3. This year, aided by federal and state grants, Lowell spent $5.9 million dollars on bilingual education; courses are offered in Spanish, Khmer, Lao, Portuguese and Vietnamese.

4. Surprisingly, most educators who work with the new immigrants believe competence in English and the maintenance of cultural identity are compatible goals.

5. "I have to understand in Vietnamese first . . . so I can translate it into English. I learn best this way."

6. "You teach children in the language they think in; then they understand the concepts. Once they understand the concepts, they can transfer these skills to a second language. I know it works. I've been doing it for 10 years and see the results."

7. "It's hard to find someone who can teach math in Korean."

8. California's recession and fiscal crisis produced a 20% drop in school funding between 1990 and 1992.

9. "Hundreds of millions of dollars are being stolen from American children who need computers, books and guards."

10. Interestingly, those on the front lines of this struggle—the teachers and the local administrators burdened by growing responsibilities and dwindling resources—have hardly any complaints about the new immigrants.

. . . .

VOCABULARY: KEEPING AN ONGOING PERSONAL VOCABULARY LIST

As you have seen, the activities in this textbook have been designed to help you help yourself with your education and your study of English outside the classroom. In keeping with this approach, this vocabulary activity—unlike those in previous chapters, which included specific words and phrases from the readings—asks you to focus exclusively on the words and phrases from "Teach Your Children Well" that *you* choose to explore.

You may want to choose words you've come across before but that still remain unclear to you; or words that seem to be used in a manner different from their more common meanings; or words whose context offers you no help when you try to determine the definition. Copy the context of each word, the sentence or phrase where the word appears. Try to determine the meaning from the context. Then provide a dictionary definition either in English or in your native language. Finally, read the article a second time, paying close attention to the words you have learned as well as the other points discussed in the previous activities.

Many students find it helpful to keep an ongoing personal vocabulary list of words and phrases they come across in their reading—inside and outside of school. Like other students, you might find that you would like to continue to keep your list long after you finish using this textbook.

Student Essays

Students are often asked to write essays in class about an important issue in the news; in fact, the placement examination that determines the appropriate level of ESL instruction for incoming college students often includes the writing of an essay on some newsworthy issue.

When asked to write an essay in class exploring the most effective way to educate students with limited English, Mei Sun from Hong Kong and Larissa Brodsky from Russia took very different positions. Later they were able to revise their essays outside of class. As you read the revised essays, pay particular attention to the evidence they cite in support of their positions.

BILINGUAL EDUCATION:
GOOD FOR THE IMMIGRANT AND GOOD FOR THE COUNTRY

(First Version)

MEI SUN

In recent years, there has been a dramatic rise in the number of peo-   1
ple immigrating to the United States. Almost none have English as a native language. Tens of thousands of these are children who will attend
American schools. How should these students be educated? The public
schools of many communities throughout the country with large immigrant populations offer bilingual education programs where students
can learn English as a second language while continuing their education in their native language. This is good not only for the immigrants; it
is also good for America.

While there may be a question as to how long an immigrant student   2
should be offered instruction outside of English, bilingual education is
especially important for those children who have only recently arrived

in the United States. A student who doesn't know the language of instruction is doomed to failure and humiliation. I have a friend who came from China several years ago with her daughter who was ten years old at the time. The little girl could not speak English. I remember that her mother told me that her daughter was so worried about going to an all-English school that she would wake up in the middle of the night complaining of stomach cramps. Sometimes she refused to go to school in the morning.

Later my friend learned of a school nearby which had a Chinese-   3
English bilingual program. In addition to receiving classes in English as a second language, the Chinese students in the school met daily with a Chinese teacher who taught them various subjects in Mandarin, the dialect of my friend. My friend's daughter loved going to that school. She not only learned English well, she got high grades in her other subjects, too. After she finished elementary school, she went to an intermediate school without a Chinese-English bilingual program. This past year, she was accepted into one of the specialized high schools in the area which requires students to have not only an excellent average, but high reading and math levels.

Because bilingual education is good for the children of immigrants, it   4
is good for America. With bilingual education programs available in the public schools, more immigrants with limited English will be able to receive an education of quality. It is my impression that immigrant students work and study very hard, often harder than the typical American student. They want to make the most of opportunities which they did not have in their countries. If they get a good education in high school they will be able to do well in college. They will become productive members of society working for themselves and in so doing working for America. The stories of immigrants successful in science and industry are well known. How many more success stories would there be if bilingual education were made even more available?

There are many Americans who are opposed to bilingual education.   5
If funds for bilingual education are cut, immigrant children will find themselves in a situation where they will be unable to do well in school and will be reluctant to attend. They will not be able to adjust to the American system of education. As a result, school districts will be wasting time and money on students who will drop out because they will not be able to succeed in classes which they hardly understand.

The stomachache of that little Chinese girl will be magnified into a   6
heartache for the entire country.

· · · · · · · · · · · · · · · · ·

RESPONSE AND ANALYSIS

1. What is the thesis of Mei's essay on how to educate students with limited English? Where in the essay is it stated? Do you agree or disagree with her position? Explain.

2. According to Mei, what are the advantages of bilingual education? The disadvantages of immersion into all-English instruction?

3. Make a list of the specific evidence that Mei cites to support her position.

4. What do you think Mei means in the conclusion to the essay when she states, "The stomachache of that little Chinese girl will be magnified into a heartache for the entire country"?

5. Has this essay affected in any way your own position on the topic? Explain.

ENGLISH ONLY

(First Version)

LARISSA BRODSKY

The most effective way to educate students with limited English is to   1
put them straight into the regular education program with native speakers of the language. Immersion of these students into a program where instruction is entirely in English will help thousands of immigrants fulfill their American dream.

Many times I read in the local papers about people who are con-   2
cerned about children growing up separated from their heritage. They are eager to see the traditional language and culture maintained. These champions of bilingual education believe that teaching immigrant students in their native language is essential to their academic and psychological well-being. They believe that immigrant children must first be taught mathematics, science, and social studies in their native language. They say that children are afraid to open up in a class dominated by English-speaking students.

When I came to the United States from Russia, I went straight into   3
the regular education program with the other American students even though my English was poor. There were not enough speakers of my language for my school to offer a bilingual program. Besides my English as a second language classes, all my other classes were in the regular

school program with the other American students. Based on my own experiences, I have come to believe that complete immersion into English instruction is the most effective way to learn English. I am thankful that I was not offered a Russian-English bilingual program. You can't learn English when a large part of your school day is spent studying in your native language.

I understand that it is not easy for students with limited English to go directly into the regular education program. I remember how hard I had to work to succeed in high school when I first came here. I would spend hours reading an assignment of a few pages from my American history textbook. I could have completed that assignment in minutes if I were reading Russian and not English. But I had to complete my homework. It was terribly frustrating to look up literally hundreds of words in my Russian-English dictionary.   4

In addition, just being with my American classmates all day in school forced me to study English harder and harder. I knew that if I wanted to have friends, I had to know their language. I remember how angry I would become at myself when I wanted to talk to my American friends about some television program I had seen the night before or about a letter I had gotten from my older sister in Russia but I could not because my English was not good enough. Or I dared not because I was so sensitive about my language skills.   5

However, I was so happy when I noticed after a few months that my English had improved substantially. I began to use my dictionary less frequently. At the end of my first year, I didn't use it much at all. Because I could understand so much of the texts I was reading, I could use the context of what I was reading to help me understand the words I did not know. You can't imagine the satisfaction I felt. The history assignment that had taken me hours, I could now complete in a quarter of the time. Maybe not as fast as if it had been in Russian, but fast enough to leave me feeling that I could succeed in college here in the United States. I also remember how happy I was when I began to talk comfortably with my friends and understand and laugh at their jokes.   6

I don't believe that I could have learned English as fast and as well as I have if I had been in a Russian-English bilingual program. It was worth the effort to work hard at the beginning immersed in English. I encourage all immigrant students to go directly into an academic program where all instruction is in English.   7

· · · · · · · · · · · · · · · ·

RESPONSE AND ANALYSIS

1. What is the thesis of Larissa's essay on how to educate students with limited English? Where in the essay is it stated? Do you agree or disagree with her position? Explain.

2. According to Larissa, what are the advantages of immersion into instruction entirely in English? The disadvantages of bilingual education?

3. Make a list of the specific evidence that Larissa cites to support her position.

4. Notice that in paragraph 2 Larissa mentions some of the arguments made by proponents of bilingual education. In your opinion, does this strengthen or weaken her essay? Explain.

5. Has this essay affected in any way your own position on the topic? Explain.

Focus on Writing: Research

As someone who has come from a language background other than English, you probably already have had personal experience with the issues involving the education of immigrants. You may have come to understand how your education has been affected by participating in a bilingual program or in a program where instruction was entirely in English. Based on your own experiences as well as those of your acquaintances, you may have formed a strong and definite position on the issue. However, you must realize that these experiences are limited and that a position on a complicated issue based exclusively on anecdotal evidence may turn out to be too simplistic. To come to a more sophisticated position, you will have to broaden your knowledge. And as you learn more about an issue, you may very well find that your position will change.

In the previous chapter you explored how to go about gathering information and writing essays based on interviewing others. The writing activities in this chapter focus on library research.

Before exploring some of the issues involved in library research, let's look at the final versions of the two essays that you have just read. Remember that these essays began as an in-class writing assignment. As you read the final versions, notice how Mei and Larissa have included other sources of information and ideas to refine and add support to their positions, making for a more sophisticated essay.

BILINGUAL EDUCATION:
GOOD FOR THE IMMIGRANT AND GOOD FOR THE COUNTRY
(Final Version)

MEI SUN

According to the United States Immigration and Naturalization Service, more than 10 million people have immigrated to the United States in the past two decades. Few have English as a native language. Hundreds of thousands of these are children who will attend American schools. How should these students be educated? The public schools of many communities throughout the country with large immigrant populations offer bilingual education programs where students can learn English as a second language while continuing their education in their native language. This is good not only for the immigrants; it is also good for America.

I recently read in an article in *Time* magazine that most teachers are in favor of bilingual education. One teacher who works in an elementary school in San Francisco summarized the advantages of bilingual education when she said, "It's really very simple. You teach children in the language they think in; then they understand the concepts. Once they understand the concepts, they can transfer these skills to a second language." Her ten years of experience have shown that the method is successful (Gray, 1993).

Yet there are many Americans who are opposed to bilingual education. They say that bilingual education isolates minority groups and that it makes the transition to speaking, reading, and writing English slower. However, there is research that contradicts this view. A recent study made by the United States Department of Education concluded that bilingual education "helps a child make a smoother and more successful transition into an all-English classroom" (Cellis, 1991).

While there may be a question as to how long an immigrant student should be offered instruction outside of English, bilingual education is especially important for those children who have only recently arrived in the United States if they are to make the transition into the American society and economy. A student who doesn't know the language of instruction is doomed to failure and humiliation. I have personally seen how bilingual education can help young students who come to the United States with limited English.

I have a friend who came from China several years ago with her daughter, who was ten years old at the time. The little girl could not speak English. I remember that her mother told me that her daughter was so worried about going to an all-English school that she would wake up in the middle of the night complaining of stomach cramps. Sometimes she refused to go to school in the morning.

Later my friend learned of a school nearby which had a Chinese-English bilingual program. In addition to receiving classes in English as a second language, the Chinese students in the school met daily with a Chinese teacher who taught them various subjects in Mandarin, the dialect of my friend. My friend's daughter loved going to that school. She not only learned English well, she got high grades in her other subjects, too. After she finished elementary school, she went to an intermediate school without a Chinese-English bilingual program. This past year, she was accepted into one of the specialized high schools in the area, which requires students to have not only an excellent average but high reading and math levels.   6

Bilingual education has a long tradition in the United States. As early as the 1840s, there were bilingual programs in Cincinnati, New York City, and other cities (Fishman, 1993). Yet some Americans claim that the country cannot afford to provide bilingual education. Recently, a candidate for governor of California claimed that because so much money was directed to bilingual education, "millions of dollars are being stolen from American children who need computers, books and guards" (Gray, 1993).   7

I believe, however, that the United States cannot afford to eliminate bilingual programs. If funds for bilingual education are cut, immigrant children will find themselves in a situation where they will be unable to do well in school, and they will be reluctant to attend. They will not be able to adjust to the American system of education. As a result, school districts will be wasting time and money on students who will drop out because they will not be able to succeed in classes which they hardly understand.   8

The stomachache of that little Chinese girl will be magnified into a heartache for the entire country.   9

References

Cellis, William. "Bilingual Education: A New Focus on Both Tongues." *New York Times,* 27 November 1991: B1.

Fishman, Joshua. "Bilingual Education." *World Book Encyclopedia,* 1993.

Gray, Paul, et al. "Teach Your Children Well." *Time,* fall 1993: 69–71.

United States Bureau of the Census. *Statistical Abstract* 1993 (113th edition). Washington, DC, 1993.

. . . .

ANALYSIS

1. In paragraph 1 of the earlier version of her essay, Mei writes, "In recent years, there has been a dramatic rise in the number of people immigrating to the United States." In the final version, she has cited specific factual information from the United States Immigration and Naturalization Service to support the claim: " . . . more than 10 million people have immigrated to the United States in the past two decades."

   Similarly, in the earlier version of her essay, Mei supports her position on bilingual education by telling of the experiences of her friend's daughter. In the final version, she includes information and ideas outside her own experiences and those of her acquaintances to give her position even more authority and support. For example, in paragraph 2, she includes an explanation from an elementary school teacher about how bilingual education works: "You teach children in the language they think in; then they understand the concepts. . . . " Later she notes that the teacher's many years of experience has shown that the method is successful.

   List the other material that Mei has added to the final version of her essay. Explain what each item contributes to the essay.

2. Besides adding material to the final version of her essay, Mei has also decided to omit items that were included in the early version. Which material has Mei decided to omit? What possible reasons might she have had for making this decision?

. . . .

GIVING CREDIT TO YOUR SOURCES

Throughout her essay, Mei notes where she has gotten her information and ideas. For example, Mei introduces the statistics about rising immigration to the United States in paragraph 1 by noting, "According to the United States Immigration and Naturalization Service. . . . " In paragraph 2, the idea that a majority of teachers favor bilingual education and the observations of the elementary school teacher are introduced with the phrase, "I recently read an article in *Time* magazine. . . . " After she has completed citing the material, Mei provides the author of the article as well as the year of its publication in parentheses (Gray, 1993).

Where else in the essay does Mei mention the source of her information and ideas?

Now look at the list of references that appears at the end of the essay. What information has Mei included there?

As you can see, in an essay that involves research, you are required to give credit to the sources of the information and ideas you use. A number of styles are acceptable, but the most common is to mention the sources of the material you are using briefly in the actual text of the essay and then provide more complete information in a list of references at the end. The rules about the appropriate way to list these sources are extremely involved. There are many good handbooks that can help you use the style that is required in each case. At this point, just be sure to include enough information so that the reader is able to locate the source of the material used in the essay.

· · · · · · · · · · · · · · · · ·

QUOTING VS. PARAPHRASING

In your previous essays, you were often confronted with the choice of using direct quotation or reported speech. Generally, if the actual words are of particular importance, you employ direct quotation; if not, you opt for reported speech. The same idea is true when you deal with research material in your essays.

In paragraph 3 of Mei's essay, for example, she uses a direct quotation from a newspaper article stating that bilingual education "helps a child make a smoother and more successful transition into an all-English classroom." Other times, however, Mei decides not to quote the exact words used in her sources; instead she chooses to *paraphrase,* or express the information and ideas in her own words. In paragraph 7, she mentions the tradition of bilingual education in the United States; notice that she uses her own words while including the source of the information (Fishman, 1993).

Go back to the list you compiled of the research material Mei has included in her essay. For each item, indicate if direct quotation or paraphrasing has been used.

Now read the revised version of Larissa's essay. Afterward, you will be able to analyze the changes she has made.

ENGLISH ONLY
(Final Version)
LARISSA BRODSKY

The most effective way to educate students with limited English is to   1
put them straight into the regular education program with native speak-

ers of the language. Immersion of these students into a program where instruction is entirely in English will help thousands of immigrants fulfill their American dream.

Many times I read in the local papers about people and teachers who   2
are concerned about children growing up separated from their heritage. They are eager to see the traditional language and culture maintained. These champions of bilingual education believe that teaching immigrant students in their native language is essential to their academic and psychological well-being. They believe that immigrant children must first be taught mathematics, science, and social studies in their native language. They say that children are afraid to open up in a class dominated by English-speaking students. One teacher in Brooklyn, New York, said of her Haitian students, "In a regular classroom they're afraid to open up. But in a bilingual classroom, they're not afraid because everybody has the same problem, so it's one happy family" (Berger, 1993).

In my apartment building there are many tenants from the Caribbean   3
and from Central and South America. After speaking with some of them, I understood that while some want their children to study in a bilingual program, many do not. One woman told me that her children already know Spanish; she wanted them to go to school to learn English. Another woman told me that her little boy was placed in a bilingual program even though he was born in the United States and could speak English. These poor women agree with the historian Arthur Schlesinger, who writes that "bilingual education retards rather than expedites the movement of Hispanic children into the English speaking world and that it promotes segregation more than integration." After all is said and done, bilingual education hurts Spanish-speaking children more than it helps them (Schlesinger, 1992).

I am thankful that I was not offered a Russian-English bilingual program when I came to the United States from Russia. You can't learn   4
English when a large part of your school day is spent studying in your native language. Because there were not enough speakers of my language for my school to offer a bilingual program, I went straight into the regular education program with the other American students even though my English was poor. Besides my English as a second language classes, all my other classes were in the regular school program with the other American students. I remember how hard I had to work to pass my classes. I would spend hours reading an assignment of a few pages from my American history textbook. I could have completed that assignment in minutes if I were reading Russian and not English.

But I had to complete my homework. It was terribly frustrating to look up literally hundreds of words in my Russian-English dictionary.

In addition, just being with my American classmates all day in 5 school forced me to study English harder and harder. I knew that if I wanted to have friends, I had to know their language. I remember how angry I would become at myself when I wanted to talk to my American friends about some television program I had seen the night before or about a letter I had gotten from my older sister in Russia but I could not because my English was not good enough. Or I dared not because I was so sensitive about my language skills.

However, I was so happy when I noticed after a few months that my 6 English had improved substantially. I began to use my dictionary less frequently. At the end of my first year, I didn't use it much at all. Because I could understand so much of the texts I was reading, I could use the context of what I was reading to help me understand the words I did not know. You can't imagine the satisfaction I felt. The history assignment that had taken me hours, I could now complete in a quarter of the time. Maybe not as fast as if it had been in Russian, but fast enough to leave me feeling that I could succeed in college here in the United States. I also remember how happy I was when I began to talk comfortably with my friends and understand and laugh at their jokes.

In contrast, I would see many of my schoolmates who studied in the 7 bilingual program interacting with other Spanish speakers throughout the day. I would pass them in the hall and notice many of their textbooks were in Spanish. How could they learn English well enough to continue their education or get a good job here in the United States? I was not surprised to read that when Con Edison, the public utility company of New York City, gave an English test to job applicants recently, not one of those who passed the test had graduated from a bilingual education program. More than 3/4 of the teachers in Los Angeles, the city with the largest population of students with limited English in the country, are opposed to bilingual education (Porter, 1990). Is it any wonder?

I don't believe that I could have learned English as fast and as well as 8 I have if I had been in a Russian-English bilingual program. It was worth the effort to work hard at the beginning immersed in English. I encourage all immigrant students to go directly into an academic program where all instruction is in English.

References

Berger, Joseph. "School Programs Assailed as Bilingual Bureaucracy." *New York Times,* 4 January 1993: A1.

Porter, Rosalie Pedalino. "Bilingual Education Trap: No English Is No Future for Our Kids." *Las Vegas Review Journal,* 13 May 1990: C1.

Schlesinger, Arthur M., Jr. *The Disuniting of America.* New York: W. W. Norton and Company, 1992.

. . . .

ANALYSIS

Identify the material that Larissa has added to the final version of her essay. For each item state the source of the material, what it contributes to the essay, and whether direct quotation or paraphrasing has been used.

. . . .

USING THE LIBRARY

It is not uncommon for students who come from abroad to feel apprehensive at the thought of using a library in the United States. Like most things in life, however, the more library research you do, the more competent you will feel. As the proverb goes, Practice makes perfect—or at least it moves you a step or two in the right direction.

Some students like to begin their research by using a general encyclopedia. While it may not give you the most current or detailed material, an encyclopedia article can provide you with a good general introduction to your topic. In addition, there are numerous specialized encyclopedias and other reference works on specific topics. For example, an important work that supplied much of the background information on the immigrant groups and other topics mentioned in this book was *The Harvard Encyclopedia of American Ethnic Groups* (ed. Stephan Thernstrom et al. [Cambridge: Harvard University Press, 1980]).

As useful as these reference works are, however, when you look for material on current issues in the news, you will probably want to focus on periodicals—newspapers, magazines, and journals—more than books. These will provide you with the most current and detailed information and ideas as well as present you with different perspectives on the issue.

There are many indexes available to help you find articles on the subject you are investigating:

- *The New York Times Index* provides a comprehensive account of the articles that appear in the newspaper. Libraries often carry the complete set of back editions on microfilm.

- *The Reader's Guide to Periodical Literature* indexes articles from hundreds of newspapers, magazines, and journals. If your library does not carry the actual issue or the microfilm of the edition you are looking for, you may have to go to a library with a more comprehensive catalogue of periodicals to find an article. But you can usually find some material that will help you even in a smaller library with fewer resources.

- With advances in technology, such as CD-ROM, there are now many indexes—updated monthly—available on computer. The computerized indexes make your search for material easier and faster; in addition, these indexes will often contain an *abstract* or summary of the article or even the complete text.

When looking through an index, let the title of the article be a diagnostic: if the title sounds promising, try to get the abstract, or the complete text of the article. Skim to determine if the article suits your purposes. However, be prepared for disappointment; the article you have chosen to explore may not contain the information or ideas you require. Even though you have spent some time and effort looking for the article, if it isn't right for your essay, don't use it. As the saying goes, "You can't force a square peg into a round hole!" You may have to look through a number of articles until you find one you can use.

Approach your research as a detective trying to solve a mystery. The detective has to explore every possible clue, many of which will prove to be irrelevant, some even misleading. However, there is usually the one clue that holds the key to the solution. The same is true of your research. You may have to look at quite a bit of material until you find what you need.

When you do find an appropriate article, it is a good idea to photocopy it, although this practice can turn out to be expensive. Almost all libraries have photocopiers; in addition, many of the microfilm projectors and computerized indexes allow you to make copies as well. Having your own copy of an article will certainly make your job easier; you can refer back to it over and over again at your leisure.

As important as all these research tools are, however, perhaps your most valuable resource is the librarian. It is the librarian's job to direct you, to help you find information, and to operate the library's hardware—its computers and microfilm projectors. Don't be reluctant to ask for help.

. . . .

CHOOSING A TOPIC

The essay assignment for this chapter differs from the others you have done so far in that it encourages you to choose your essay topic. Specifically, you are asked to choose a controversial issue in the news and to express your position on it. In keeping with the themes you have explored to this point, you might want to choose an issue that relates to the immigrant experience.

Whatever issue you choose to write about, make sure that it is sufficiently specific so that you can explore it adequately in a relatively short essay. The theme of "immigration" or "immigration to the United States" is so broad that you could not expect to cover all the issues related to it in a book, let alone a relatively short essay. Look at the following issues suggested by other students. Notice that each is specific enough to allow the writer to explore the issue and express a position on it in an essay.

- Should immigration to the United States be restricted?
- What should be done about illegal immigration?
- Should English be the official language of the United States?
- Do immigrants help or hurt the American economy?
- What can be done to help the children of immigrants overcome the challenge of moving to the United States?
- What do immigrants contribute to American society?
- What should American policy be toward accepting political refugees?
- What can be done to help immigrants adapt to life in the United States?

There are many other issues you may wish to investigate. Perhaps the most important consideration when selecting a topic is also the simplest: choose one that interests you.

Essay Writing

. . . .

GENERATING IDEAS

As you have seen, the more knowledge you bring to your reading and writing, the more accessible they become. The more you know about a subject, the more you will understand reading about it and the easier it is to write about it. When writing about an issue in the news, you might want to begin by examining what you already know before you search for information and ideas in other sources.

Use the following suggestions as a guide to help you explore the information and ideas you may already have about the topic you have chosen. But as always, feel free to consider anything related to the subject. A sample student response from the issue explored in this chapter accompanies each suggestion.

a. Identify the specific issue and examine why it is newsworthy.

Example

In recent years, there has been a dramatic rise in the number of people immigrating to the United States. Almost none have English as a native language. Tens of thousands of these are children who will attend American schools. How should students with limited English be educated?

b. Define words and phrases that are central to your investigation.

Examples

Bilingual education provides students with the opportunity to study their native language and culture while receiving instruction in English as a second language. Many bilingual programs offer content area subjects, such as social studies, mathematics, and science, in languages other than English.

Transitional bilingual education in the United States provides bilingual instruction until the student is able to succeed in an all-English environment.

Some bilingual programs teach English to students with backgrounds in other languages yet also encourage them to maintain their native language and culture. These are called *bilingual maintenance* programs. Still other bilingual programs attempt to give American students proficiency in a language other than English.

c. Discuss your personal connection with the issue.

Examples

I have a friend who came from China several years ago with her daughter, who was ten years old at the time. The little girl could not speak English. I remember that her mother told me that her daughter was so worried about going to an all-English school that she would wake up in the middle of the night complaining of stomach cramps. Sometimes she refused to go to school in the morning.

I understand that it is not easy for students with limited English to go directly into the regular education program. I remember how hard I had to work to succeed in high school when I first came here. I would spend hours reading an assignment of a few pages from my American history textbook. I could have completed that assignment in minutes if I were reading Russian and not English. But I had to complete my homework. It was terribly frustrating to look up literally hundreds of words in my Russian-English dictionary.

d. Refer to relevant information and ideas you have come across in your reading.

Example

Many times I read in the local paper about people who are concerned about children growing up separated from their heritage. They are eager to see the traditional language and culture maintained. . . .

e. Draft a thesis statement of your position on the issue. Clearly state reasons that support your position.

Examples

The public schools of many communities with large immigrant populations offer bilingual education programs where students can learn English as a second language while continuing their education in their native language. This is good not only for the immigrants; it is also good for America.

A student who doesn't know the language of instruction is doomed to failure and humiliation.

The most effective way to educate students with limited English is to put them straight into the regular education program with native speakers of the language.

You can't learn English when a large part of your school day is spent studying in your native language.

f. Respond to arguments made in favor of the opposing position.

Examples

There are many Americans who are opposed to bilingual education. If funds for bilingual education are cut, immigrant children will find themselves in a situation where they will be unable to do well in school and will be reluctant to attend. They will not be able to adjust to the American system of education. As a result, school districts will be wasting time and money on students who will drop out because they will not be able to succeed in classes that they hardly understand.

These champions of bilingual education believe that teaching immigrant students in their native language is essential to their academic and psychological well-being. They believe that immigrant children must first be taught mathematics, science, and social studies in their native language. They say that children are afraid to open up in a class dominated by English-speaking children. Experience shows otherwise.

g. Include any recommendations you may have and discuss their expected outcomes.

Examples

I encourage all immigrant students to go directly into an academic program where all instruction is in English. Immersion of these students into a program where instruction is entirely in English will help thousands of immigrants fulfill their American dream.

With bilingual education available in the public schools, more immigrants with limited English will be able to receive an education of quality. . . . If they get a good education in high school they will be able to do well in college. They will become productive members of society working for themselves and in so doing working for America.

These suggestions are general enough to help you generate ideas for whatever issue you decide to write about. Remember, however, that as with the other times you have engaged in activities to help you generate ideas, you will probably end up including some in your essay while omitting others. You must also decide how to organize the ideas you decide to include. While many writers like to prepare an outline before they begin writing, others prefer to write an early draft and work on an outline as they change the organization during the revision.

. . . .

ASSIGNMENT

This essay requires you to discuss your position on a controversial issue in the news that you have researched. You might find it helpful to begin by generating some of your own ideas and organizing them into an essay before you go on to your library research. Even if you find that your position changes as a result of the material you uncover, having a preliminary version of your essay can provide you with a starting point from which to operate. As you become more experienced, you may decide to go directly to doing library research without writing the preliminary version. The steps of the two approaches are summarized below.

Writing an Essay about Your Position on an Issue in the News

Two Approaches

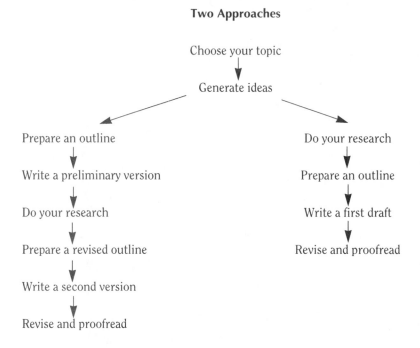

Choose your topic

Generate ideas

Prepare an outline

Write a preliminary version

Do your research

Prepare a revised outline

Write a second version

Revise and proofread

Do your research

Prepare an outline

Write a first draft

Revise and proofread

Like Mei and Larissa, include direct quotations or paraphrase the information and ideas you find in your research to support your position. Remember to mention the source of the material you use briefly in the text of the essay and then provide a more detailed list of the sources at the end. After you have written an early draft of your essay, share it with a classmate who does not agree with your position. As you are forced to defend your position, you may come up with possible revisions to your essay that would make it even more successful.

AFTERWORD

With every ending there comes a new beginning. As this semester winds down and as you prepare to close this textbook for perhaps the final time, understand that your education and your study of English continue.

Think back to the beginning of the semester. Skim this textbook and your own work once again—the readings, the essays, your journal. Surely you must feel that your English is better today than it was just several months ago. Perhaps you also have new understanding into the immigrant experience as you and others have lived it. And while the progress you have made must be a source of great satisfaction to you, keep in mind that further into the future, your English will be even better and your understanding even more profound.

It is said that a journey of a thousand miles begins with a single step. Whatever your intended destination, it is hoped that this semester and this textbook have helped you move a little in that direction. Good luck.

ACKNOWLEDGMENTS

INDEX